Field Work in
Urban Geography

Field Work in Urban Geography

K. Briggs B A

Head of the Geography Department,
Canon Slade Grammar School, Bolton

illustrated by
Crispin Fisher

Oliver & Boyd

Oliver & Boyd
Croythorn House
23 Ravelston Terrace
Edinburgh EH3 3TJ
(A Division of Longman Group Ltd.)

ISBN 0 05 002200 8

First impression 1971
Second impression 1975

Set in 'Monophoto' Ehrhardt 11/13pt
and Grot 215 & 216 and
Printed in Hong Kong by
Dai Nippon Printing Co., (Hong Kong) Ltd

Acknowledgment

The plan suggested for the survey of industries on pages 20, 23 and 47 is partly based
upon the categories of the Standard Industrial Classification which are indicated in
brackets: I1 (IV,V,VI,VII,VIII,IX and XIII), I2 (X,XI,XII), I3 (III) and I4 (XIV snd XV).
The shop classification suggested on pages 46, 64 and 65, and used in Tables 1 and 2,
is partly based upon the following headings of the Standard Industrial Classification:
820 (1) – (S1, S2 and S7), 820(2) – (S3 to S8), 820(3) – (S9), 820(4) – (S10 to S12),
820(5) – (S13 to S15, and S16 with modification), 820(6) – (S17 to S21 and S24),
820(7) – (S25 to S27), 883 – (S30), 886 – (S35), 888 – (S32), 889 – (S31).
The author and publishers are indebted to H.M. Stationery Office for permission to
use parts of the Standard Industrial Classification as described above.

Contents

1 Field Work in Urban Geography

The Meaning of Urban Geography

The purpose of field work in urban geography is to obtain a fuller understanding of the towns in which we live. By field work we can learn at first-hand about the geography of a town.

Urban geography is concerned with the structure, functions and interrelationships of towns and cities. The structure of a town is its physical form, expressed in the types and arrangement of its buildings. Most towns have developed from a small nucleus over a long period of time and are continuing to expand into the surrounding rural areas. The successive stages in this development may be seen in the nature and form of buildings and street patterns. The major function of towns is to serve as places where people live, but some parts of towns are devoted to manufacturing industries, shopping centres, parks and recreation grounds and other functions. All these different parts of towns are linked together in very complex ways, often by journeys which people make from one part of the town to another, such as journeys from homes to work or from homes to shopping or entertainment centres. No town exists in isolation. Very complex links exist between any town and many other towns and villages. By field work in urban geography we try to investigate these characteristics and interrelationships.

The task of the urban planner is to design towns which are able to carry out their urban functions in the most efficient way possible. Any decision made by a planner is bound to affect the people who live in the town. Hence, it is important that the townspeople should understand the problems and aims of the planner and co-operate with him in improving the urban environment. Field work in urban geography leads to a better understanding of the urban environment so that there may be more fruitful co-operation between the townspeople and the planner.

Much of geography is inevitably second-hand and has to be learned from investigations which have been made by other people. Field work in urban geography gives the opportunity for any student to carry out a piece of original geographical research. In performing field work the student has to make careful observations of the details of the town and record them accurately and precisely. He is then able to study his material and formulate his conclusions. This is the finest type of self-education.

A good idea of the geographical characteristics of a town may be obtained by taking a bus ride along a main road from the outskirts to the town centre. Many main roads in many different towns in Britain show broadly the same characteristics. Each is rather like a cross-section through a town. It should be remembered however that some towns, such as New Towns and towns which are crowded closely together to form a conurbation, may not possess these characteristics.

One approaches the town through a rural area along a road which usually has a speed limit of 65 km/h or no speed limit at all. The road may be a dual carriageway; traffic lights are rare, many major intersections being in the form of roundabouts. Few roads lead off the main roads, and the ones that do have usually been called 'avenues', 'roads' or 'lanes' rather than 'streets'.

Much of the land on each side of the road is farming land, but there may also be golf courses, large parks and playing fields. Industry may be present in the form of modern, single-storey factories set in gardens. Farmhouses may be seen, and sometimes large old houses, set in extensive grounds. In some cases, these houses have been turned into hospitals, nursing homes, schools and other institutions requiring plenty of space. Modern detached and semi-detached houses may be seen stretching along the road in 'ribbon' form with farm land beyond their back garden fences. Alternatively, the houses may be arranged in compact modern housing estates.

The road may sometimes pass through a village, often consisting of a group of older cottages near a crossroads. Here, the narrow street, with buildings set well forward, and traffic lights at the crossroads, may lead to traffic congestion. All this is the outer area of the town and its character is very easily recognized.

Towards the town centre, the surroundings begin to change considerably. The road has a 50 km/h speed limit; many zebra crossings appear, and there are many more roads (now called 'streets') leading off the main route. The main road is bordered by rows of terraced houses which usually continue along the side streets as far as one can see. These houses are closely packed together, so the population density of this area is high. Hence, one finds more people on the pavements and crossing the road, and there are other driving hazards which were not encountered on the outskirts of the town, such as parked cars and delivery vans and many more bus stops. Schools have small concrete playgrounds instead of grassy playing fields, and public houses are found at street corners. Often there are rows of shops lining the road, particularly near important road junctions where banks also begin to appear. Closer to the centre of the town, the quality of housing begins to change. Many houses are in a very poor state of repair and shops are often dilapidated or empty. There may be tall blocks of flats built on land formerly occupied by old property. A great deal of industry exists in close proximity to the houses. This is the inner zone of the town and, again, there is no difficulty in recognizing it.

In the centre of the town, there is often a dramatic change in the townscape. Traffic congestion becomes suddenly much more severe and traffic lights are found at many junctions. Pavements are crowded with pedestrians. Here, no houses are seen; the street frontages are dominated by shops, offices and hotels. Many large banks are found in the shopping areas. Very large shops such as Woolworth's and Marks and Spencer's, department stores and branches of national multiple shops such as Smith's, Timpson's and Burton's are located in this central part of the town. Here, too, is the Town Hall, together with other local and national government offices. Entertainment facilities exist in the form of theatres and cinemas and there are often many restaurants. The railway station and the bus station are usually here, but there are few open spaces apart from public gardens and car parks. These characteristics are typical of the central area of the town which is distinguished from the rest of the town by an almost complete absence of residential property.

Fig. 1 is an example of a simple survey of a main road leading into Bolton, which illustrates some of the features of urban geography outlined above. Some of the material was obtained on a journey along Blackburn Road and this was supplemented by a study of the 1:10560 Ordnance Survey map (six inches to one mile).

Blackburn Road runs from the northern outskirts of Bolton to the town centre, cutting across the west-east trending river valleys so that it has a broadly undulating profile. For most of its length, however, the road runs along a fairly level plateau at a height of 100 m – 130 m above sea level. The three zones of a town described above are clearly shown. The outer zone extends as far inwards as Bar Lane, where it is succeeded quite sharply by the inner zone. Finally, near St. George's Road, the central area begins.

Several quite important roads meet Blackburn Road at busy junctions. Crompton Way is a ring road built comparatively recently which permits east-bound traffic from Blackburn Road and Belmont Road to by-pass the town centre of Bolton. It continues eastwards roughly as an arc of a circle, generally following the junction between the outer zone and the inner zone of Bolton. Halliwell Road and Belmont Road are important roads leading towards more recently developed residential districts, and Belmont Road forms a major route to Preston. Most of Blackburn Road is quite definitely urban in character, but towards the Darwen Road end, certain rural characteristics begin to appear. In fact, during the summer months, the flow of traffic between Eagley Brook and Darwen Road is regularly interrupted to allow a herd of cows to cross the road at milking time!

As a simple introduction to urban geography, the information provided above and in fig. 1 should be studied carefully and the exercises at the end of this chapter attempted.

Another major aspect of field work in urban geography, in addition to the pattern of the townscape, is the pattern of the links which exist between the town and its surrounding countryside and neighbouring towns. Part of the purpose of a town is to provide various services for the people who live in the town itself and in surrounding smaller towns and villages.

It is well known that on market days the centre of a town is crowded with people who have travelled in to do their shopping. Some of these may have walked from their homes in the inner zone of the town; others may have travelled by bus or car from homes in the outer zone. Many may have made longer journeys from villages and other towns several kilometres away. If it were possible to discover the locations of the homes of all these shoppers, a map could be drawn which would show the area for which the town provides shopping and market services. Survey and mapping methods for this type of study are discussed later.

Similarly, many people travel to the town for purposes of entertainment, perhaps to attend theatres or football matches. Students travel into a town to attend a secondary school, a technical college, or meetings of the local branch of the Geographical Association.

The area from which people come to obtain the services provided by the town is known as the town's sphere of influence or urban field. The patterns of a town's sphere of influence are much more complicated than one might expect at first. They will be dealt with in chapters eight and nine.

Relief section

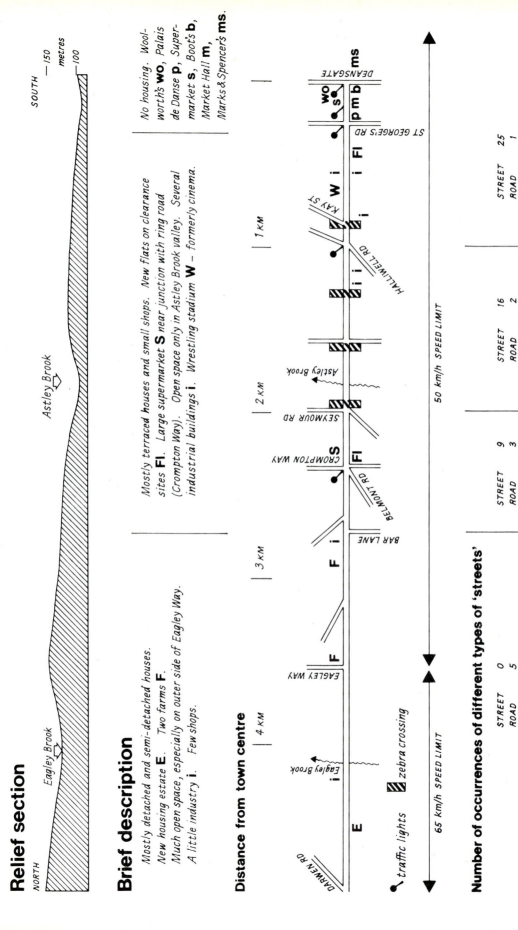

NORTH SOUTH

metres —150 —100

Eagley Brook   Astley Brook

Brief description

Mostly detached and semi-detached houses. New housing estate E. Two farms F. Much open space, especially on outer side of Eagley Way. A little industry i. Few shops.

Mostly terraced houses and small shops. New flats on clearance sites Fl. Large supermarket S near junction with ring road (Crompton Way). Open space only in Astley Brook valley. Several industrial buildings i. Wrestling stadium W – formerly cinema.

No housing. Woolworth's wo, Palais de Danse p, Supermarket s, Boot's b, Market Hall m, Marks & Spencer's ms.

Distance from town centre

DARWEN RD   EAGLEY WAY   BAR LANE   BELMONT RD   CROMPTON WAY   SEYMOUR RD   HALLIWELL RD   KAY ST   ST GEORGE'S RD   DEANSGATE

● traffic lights   ▨ zebra crossing

Eagley Brook   Astley Brook

65 km/h SPEED LIMIT   50 km/h SPEED LIMIT

Number of occurrences of different types of 'streets'

STREET 0	STREET 9	STREET 16	STREET 25
ROAD 5	ROAD 3	ROAD 2	ROAD 1
AVENUE 6	AVENUE 0	AVENUE 0	AVENUE 0
LANE 3	LANE 1	LANE 0	LANE 1
OTHERS 2	OTHERS 2	OTHERS 0	OTHERS 1
TOTAL 16	TOTAL 15	TOTAL 18	TOTAL 28

Fig. 1 Field and Map Study of Blackburn Road, Bolton

General Techniques of Field Work in Urban Geography

a) The Use of Modern Maps

The most useful Ordnance Survey maps for field work in urban geography are those on scales of 1:2500 (25·344 inches to 1 mile) and 1:1250 (50·688 inches to 1 mile). These maps show the outlines of buildings and the plots of land surrounding them in very great detail. They also show a certain amount of very useful geographical information such as the functions of some of the larger buildings and areas of ground at the time of the survey. Information is provided, for example, about the general types of industry carried on in the larger industrial buildings, and the locations of schools, churches, theatres, garages, large office buildings, post offices and banks. Since the Ordnance Survey map one has to use may be very much out of date, (many are ten years and some up to sixty years out of date) this information is not entirely reliable. Another limitation of these maps is that they fail to provide data on the use, appearance and age of the great majority of the buildings in the town.

As in other types of geographical field work, the task of the field worker is to add information to the Ordnance Survey map. The map itself is just a framework upon which he records his detailed observations.

b) Recording Geographical Information

In carrying out a study of the character and functions of a town, the field worker must make a record of all relevant information. This involves recording information on a map against the position of every building. It is usually not possible, because of lack of space on the map, to write this information in full, so it is necessary, in performing field work, to record information in some form of shorthand. This shorthand system should be as detailed as possible so that the maximum amount of information is collected during a session of field work. This means that when the follow-up work begins afterwards, it should not be necessary to return to the field for extra details. Examples of shorthand systems useful in field work in urban geography are supplied in the following chapters.

When the field work is complete, the shorthand symbols are changed into systems of colours and symbols to produce a permanent record of the field work. Afterwards, using this raw material, many different exercises may be carried out. One of the commonest of these is to divide the town into a number of 'urban regions'. Certain areas of a town have a general uniformity of character and function and these may contrast with other areas within the town. The geographer tries to recognize the shape and extent of these contrasting urban regions and in this way he may come to understand the complete town.

c) The Use of Air Photographs

Air photographs give a most vivid impression of the geography of a town. On a photograph one has the advantage of seeing the town as it actually exists – the various kinds of residential and industrial buildings, the roads, the railway sidings, the parks and other open spaces. In contrast, the Ordnance Survey map merely represents these features by means of symbols.

Ideally, air photographs should be studied in conjunction with the Ordnance Survey map of the same area. The air photograph helps to bring the map to life, and the map helps in the identification of the nature of certain areas shown on the photograph.

Before commencing the study of a town,

it is an excellent idea to obtain a number of
air photographs and to compare these with
the corresponding Ordnance Survey maps.
Similarly, when the urban study is complete,
one should look again at the air photographs
and compare them with the completed
field maps.

d) The Use of Old Maps

It is a most interesting field activity to go out
armed with an old map of a town and to
compare the present townscape with what it
must have been like perhaps a hundred
years ago. Towns are continually changing
and the present appearance of a town is the
result of the accumulation of the products of
human activity in the past. The geographer
is interested in relics of former patterns of
settlement which are 'fossilized' in the
present townscape.

Ordnance Survey maps are usually available from about the middle of the nineteenth
century onwards, and it is possible to obtain
a series of such maps to illustrate the
evolution of a town (figs. 2a, b and c). In
addition to Ordnance Survey maps, one can
obtain copies of tithe maps which show
former settlement, road and field patterns.
Many ancient maps of certain towns, of
eighteenth century or earlier date, are also
available. Usually one's local reference library and county records office will supply
helpful information.

Figs. 2a, b and c illustrate the growth, over
a period of about one hundred and twenty
years, of Astley Bridge – located about three
kilometres north of the centre of Bolton.

In 1845 (fig. 2a), the main road pattern,
consisting of Blackburn Road, Belmont
Road and Ashworth Lane (Ashworth's Lane)
had been established. There were two clusters
of settlement: one near the junction of
Blackburn Road and Belmont Road (Hills

Fold), and the other a short distance to the
south (Astley Bridge). These settlements were
surrounded by fields amongst which were
several scattered, isolated buildings and small
groups of buildings such as Sharples Hall
(A 1), Sweetloves (B 2), High Lawn (C 3),
Oldhams (D 4) and The Thorns (E 5). St.
Paul's Church (F 6) was also situated in the
fields. At this time, it is clear that Astley
Bridge was a rural settlement.

By 1890 (fig. 2b), a considerable amount of
industry had been established in Astley
Bridge. Several mills had appeared, mostly in
the space between the two clusters of settlement. The original nuclei of the settlement
pattern had been extended by the building of
terraced houses. Chapels, schools, a cemetery
and an orphanage had also appeared. By now,
Astley Bridge was a small industrial settlement. Large areas of farm land still existed
in the district, but the settlement was taking
on a distinctly urban character.

By 1969 (fig. 2c), further areas of terraced
housing, extending as far north as Bar Lane
(A 1) and Ashworth Lane, had been added to
the settlement pattern. Two new major
roads had appeared, running west and
east from the junction of Blackburn
Road and Belmont Road. These were Moss
Bank Way (B 2) running westwards, cutting
across a line of older housing at Sharples
Park (C 3), and Crompton Way, running
eastwards. Ribbon growth of modern housing had taken place along Crompton Way.
Other areas of modern housing had grown up
to the west of Belmont Road, between Belmont Road and Blackburn Road, and along
Ashworth Lane. By this time more industry had appeared in the form of mills on
the east side of Blackburn Road (D 4) and
near Holly Street (D 5). By now, Astley
Bridge had acquired a distinctly urban character, with farm land only surviving in the
north-west and north-east of the map area.

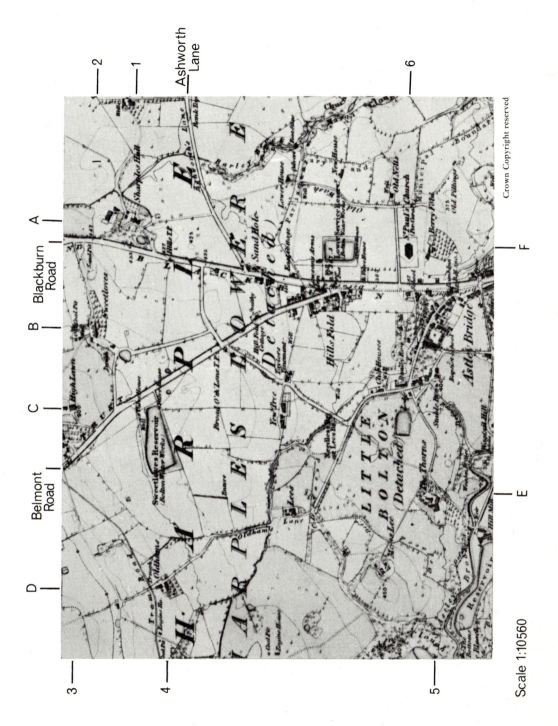

2

1

Ashworth Lane

6

A

Blackburn Road

B

C

Belmont Road

D

3

4

E

5

F

Scale 1:10560

Fig. 2a   Astley Bridge – 1845

Fig. 2b Astley Bridge — 1890

Scale 1:10560

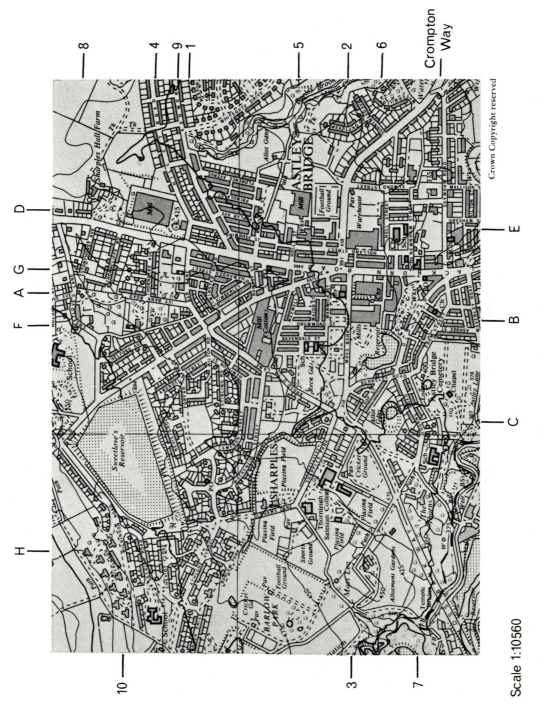

Scale 1:10560

Fig. 2c   Astley Bridge – 1969

At the present day, field work in the Astley Bridge district, aided by these maps (figs. 2a, b and c) will allow the observer to recognize that the present character of the settlement is composed of many different ingredients, some of which are relics of the 1845 and the 1890 patterns described above.

This kind of personal investigation of the make-up of an urban area can be carried out in any town.

From studying this material about Astley Bridge, ideas will be gained which can be applied in other areas. It is a useful exercise to study this material and to answer the questions at the end of this chapter.

e) Interviews

Sometimes it is possible to obtain much useful geographical information about a town by means of interviews. It is always necessary to arrange these well before the date of the survey. A letter should explain clearly the purpose of the survey and exactly what aspects of the town are being investigated. If this procedure is carefully carried out, most people are extremely willing to help. Interviews may be classified roughly as follows:

i) Local Government Officials

These are approached at either the Town Hall or the council offices. They almost always show great interest in an urban survey and are usually pleased to receive a copy of the results. They may make available for inspection the results of various surveys which they themselves have carried out and they are often prepared to discuss their plans for dealing with problems which have arisen in the town, such as traffic congestion, slum clearance, etc. This kind of information is very important in a geographical urban survey. Some large towns have an officer who is directly concerned with the industrial structure of the town. He will probably be willing to discuss changes in the types of industry in the town, changes in the level of unemployment, plans for encouraging new industries to set up in the town, etc.

ii) Industrialists

A great deal of most valuable information may be derived from a direct approach to industrial concerns. Industrialists usually wish to explain in great detail all the industrial processes carried out on their premises. This will often be most interesting, but it is important to try to obtain geographical information as well. The following is a brief outline of the kind of information which may be available.

Buildings and Site. It is important to know whether the buildings were erected for the purpose of carrying on the present industry. If the buildings were originally used by a different industry, then their site and layout may be more related to the needs of the previous industry than the present one. In this case, enquiries should be made concerning the problems the firm faced when it moved in and the kinds of modifications which had to be made. Many engineering works in the Bolton area occupy former bleach works or cotton mills whose sites and buildings were originally selected in terms of the needs of bleaching and cotton manufacturing. In some cases, the firm may have occupied the site for many years and it may be possible to inspect and copy old plans of the site and the layout of the factory.

Power Supply. It is interesting to investigate the history of the kinds of power supply which have been used by the firm. In many towns there are a great many industrial concerns dotted along river valleys. This is often because the factories were built at a time when water power was used. When water power went out of use, many firms moved to other premises but in cases where the original buildings were in sound condition, firms continued to occupy them. Relics of the water power era may sometimes be seen on the present site in the form of storage reservoirs, water channels, and, occasionally, the remains of an old wheelhouse. Sketches should be made of these layouts.

Labour Supply. Any industrial enterprise provides work for some of the town's population and thus makes an important contribution to the geographical character of the town. It may be possible to make a map of the locations of the homes of the workpeople which will be useful when assessing the sphere of influence of the town.

Products and Raw Materials. Information may be available concerning the destinations of manufactured products and the sources of raw materials. This may contribute further towards determining the sphere of influence of the town. The type of transport used for products and raw materials may have influenced the siting of the factory. Sawmills using timber transported by sea, for example, are often sited near docks. The type of transport used may have changed in a similar way to the type of power supply. A site which formerly derived an advantage through being on the banks of a canal, along which raw materials were carried, may now suffer a disadvantage because it is badly situated in relation to railways or main roads.

iii) Others
Further information concerning the sphere of influence of the town may be obtained by means of interviews. It may be possible to draw maps of the delivery areas of large shops, laundries or bakeries, or the distribution area of the local newspaper, etc., by using information gained from interviews with the firm or shop concerned. The headmaster of a secondary school in the town may supply information about the locations of the homes of its pupils.

f) Questionnaires

It is possible to discover a great deal about the sphere of influence of a town by conducting short street interviews with people who are visiting the town for purposes of shopping or entertainment. In this case, a standard questionnaire is needed. If this is not too long, most people are willing to cooperate. (Examples of questionnaires are given later.) The questionnaire, if planned very carefully and kept as short as possible, will produce an enormous amount of information.

Exercises

Refer to fig. 1 for Questions 1-10. Refer to fig. 2 for Questions 11-15.

1 For how many kilometres along Blackburn Road from the town centre of Bolton is there a 50 km/h speed limit?

2 How far is the nearest farm from the centre of the town?

3 In which part of Blackburn Road would you expect to find most public houses?

4   Why are the zebra crossings concentrated between Seymour Road and Kay Street?

5   In which part of Blackburn Road would you expect to find most dilapidated property and empty shops?

6   Contrast the locations of the two supermarkets. Suggest the advantages that might be possessed by each.

7   Which of the industrial enterprises shown would you expect to be a bleach works, requiring large amounts of water?

8   What evidence is there to show that there has been a recent expansion of building into the farm land along Blackburn Road?

9   Arrange the following stretches of Blackburn Road in their probable order of traffic density. Give reasons for your choice.
a) Crompton Way – Seymour Road, (b) Halliwell Road – Kay Street, (c) Eagley Brook–Eagley Way, (d) St. George's Road – Deansgate.

10   Choose a road leading from the outskirts to the centre of your town. Walk or ride along it and complete a survey like fig. 1. Compare your result with fig. 1. Also, carry out similar surveys along other roads leading into your town to discover in what ways they are similar and different. Try to account for these similarities and differences.

11   Locate the following streets on fig. 2c: Nell Street (E 6), Thorns Road (C7), Sweetloves Lane (F8), Thornydyke Avenue (G4) and Hillcot Road (D9). By reference to figs. 2a and b, explain the origin of these street names.

12   The school in the far north of fig. 2c is known as High Lawn School. Explain the origin of its name.

13   The council estate in the north-west of fig. 2c is known as Oldhams Estate. Explain the origin of its name.

14   What evidence is there that Old Road (B7 on fig. 2c) is in fact very old?

15   Estimate the dates at which the following groups of houses shown on fig. 2c were built:
a) the south side of Bar Lane (A1),
b) the south side of Sharples Park (C 3),
c) Sweetloves Lane (F 8).

2 The Field Study of the Morphology of a Town

General Principles

The arrangement of the buildings (settlement pattern) and the functions (use of the land) in a town are together referred to as the town's morphology. Both aspects of urban morphology exhibit interesting patterns which can be observed and studied in the field.

Many towns originated as small settlements which were founded in a particular place because of certain obvious advantages. A great number of settlements were founded near a place where a bridge crossed a river. Even today a river is often a serious barrier to movement and quite often several different roads lead towards a bridge. The bridging point of a river was therefore a focus of movement across the countryside and hence a good place to establish a settlement. Many other towns grew up around a castle which was built in a particular place because it could be defended easily. The advantages which a settlement derives from its detailed position at the bridging point of a river or on the summit of a hill are known as advantages of site.

Long ago, there were many small settlements located where advantages of site existed. These settlements provided services of various kinds for the surrounding countryside. They had to be only a few kilometres apart because transport facilities were extremely poor and it was impossible for people who lived in the countryside to travel any great distance to visit one of these settlements. Thus the spheres of influence of these small towns were very small. All the urban functions of these early towns were crowded together in a small space: houses for the townspeople, industrial concerns, shops, etc. Some towns were surrounded by defensive walls in medieval times and all buildings were crowded into the walled area. Outside the walls there was a very sudden change to a rural area. Town and country could be clearly distinguished from one another.

When modern transport facilities, such as railways, better roads, buses and cars, appeared, movement became easier so the possible spheres of influence of towns became larger. This meant that some towns carried on a greater amount of trade and therefore grew larger. Some early settlements, on the other hand, were unable to take advantage of the improved transport facilities and hardly changed in size.

Many towns did take advantage of the new transport facilities and expanded rapidly into the surrounding countryside. Norwich, for example, had been confined for centuries within its medieval walls and suddenly, in the nineteenth century, expanded beyond them. Also, in many towns, factory industry developed. This required large numbers of workpeople living fairly near the factories, so industrial towns grew. As transport facilities continued to improve, towns expanded further and further into the surrounding countryside. Former outlying villages were enveloped by this urban growth and incorporated into the town. Eventually, towns expanded so much that they began to join with other towns to create continuously built-up areas known as conurbations.

The pattern of expansion of towns was not a regular one. Towns did not grow like expanding circles of ripples in a pond. Very often the pattern of urban expansion was influenced by the presence of earlier roads and various physical features of the landscape. When railways came they often created barriers to the expansion of the town and guided it in certain directions.

Fig. 3 is an example of modern urban growth. It shows the various stages in the northward expansion of Bolton. This is an area of gently undulating plateau at a height of 90m to 130m, but the rivers flow in steep sided valleys about thirty metres below the level of the low plateau. In 1845, the settlement pattern consisted of a number of hamlets, some at road junctions, others on the sides of the deeply incised valleys. The nucleus of Bolton itself lay about a kilometre to the south. Roads ran along the easy gradients of the low plateau. Crompton Way had not been built. By 1890, the northward expansion of Bolton had enveloped the hamlets at the junctions of Halliwell Road and Blackburn Road, and Tonge Moor Road and Thicketford Road, and was advancing along the main north-south roads towards Astley Bridge in the west and Castle Hill in the east. During the twentieth century, a great deal of further expansion has taken place, but even as late

as 1951 the valley floors remained almost empty. Most of the developments along the Eagley Brook and Astley Brook valleys are industrial enterprises. Thus it is clear that the northward expansion of Bolton has been strongly influenced by relief features (the steep sided valleys) and the road pattern.

Over a period of time, as towns expanded, different settlement patterns were created in the detailed arrangement of houses and streets. Fig. 4 illustrates two contrasting patterns found in north Bolton. In the latter part of the nineteenth century, large areas of terraced housing (fig. 4a) were created in the area labelled A in fig. 3. In the twentieth century, a less dense settlement pattern in which houses have gardens (fig. 4b) has been created in the area labelled B in fig. 3.

The small town of Settle, in the upper Ribble valley in the West Riding of Yorkshire, is another example of a town which has contrasting settlement patterns. The town has expanded generally from Upper Settle in the south-east towards Settle Bridge in the north-west (fig. 5). Settlement patterns dating from at least the seventeenth century are found in Upper Settle and near the Market Place. At Upper Settle, buildings are grouped irregularly around a village green; near the Market Place there is a labyrinth of narrow passages (known locally as ginnels) and small enclosed yards. In the nineteenth century, building took place west of the railway line in the form of terraced rows of houses aligned along the ancient Kirkgate and the newer Church Street.

Most towns have been growing for a considerable length of time. During this time, older houses have become obsolete, so that, in the central part of a town, buildings have had to be demolished. At the same time, new ones have been built on the outskirts. The replacement of decaying areas of old

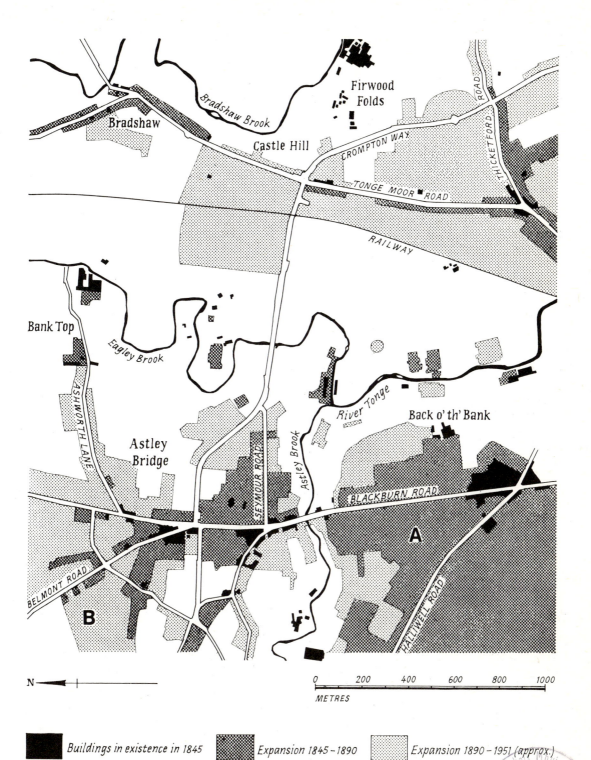

Fig. 3   The Growth of North Bolton between 1845 and 1951

a. Terraced housing

b. Council estate

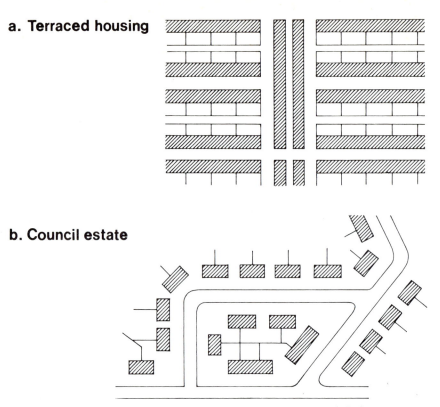

Fig. 4   Examples of Urban Settlement Patterns in North Bolton

C. Ribbon pattern

B. Ginnel pattern

A. Village green cluster

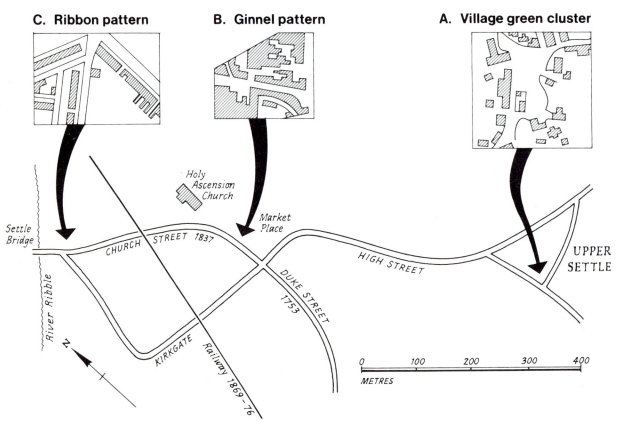

Fig. 5   Examples of Urban Settlement Patterns in Settle

housing near town centres is referred to as urban renewal. In many towns, the existence of a zone of houses 100 to 120 years old near the town centre is a serious planning problem.

During the expansion of a town, there is a tendency for the different functions which the town performs to come to occupy different areas within the town.

Most of a town's area is usually devoted to the homes of its inhabitants – the residential function. In the original nucleus, and often when the town was growing during the nineteenth century, houses and factories were placed very close together. In these districts it may be impossible to distinguish clear residential areas from areas devoted to other urban functions. This type of arrangement may be seen in Bolton's area of nineteenth century development between Blackburn Road and Halliwell Road and south-west of Halliwell Road (fig. 3). Here, many mills are dotted about in a mass of houses (fig. 6). Though the main concentrations of shops are along the main roads, this area also possesses a large number of small shops (commonly grocers or off-licences) which are usually situated at street corners. Urban functions are inextricably mixed.

As the town continued to grow after the nineteenth century, quite large areas became devoted almost entirely to the function of residence. This can be seen in the Tonge Moor Road district (fig. 6). Here, settlement which is mostly later than 1890 (fig. 3) consists almost entirely of residential property, and there is very little industry. It is well known that large modern housing estates have few industrial enterprises, shops or entertainment facilities. Many modern houses are even great distances away from a public house. Thus, it is possible to distinguish certain areas of towns which are devoted to the function of residence. It is

even possible to recognize various distinct types of residential areas. First of all, there is an obvious division in ownership between council estates and private estates, which tend to occupy different parts of a town. Then again, residential areas of different status may be recognized. There are, for example, those districts which are called by estate agents 'highly residential areas', where expensive houses and large gardens with many trees are found. In strong contrast are the slum areas of older property, towards the town centre, where demolition is taking place. One even finds that particular residential areas tend to be occupied by roughly the same kind of people. It is common to find people who work in similar occupations and who earn roughly the same wages living in the same area. One would normally expect to find, for example, industrial managers, manual workers, and coloured immigrant populations occupying different parts of a town's residential areas.

Other parts of a town may be devoted almost entirely to industry. In fig. 6, an industrial zone can easily be recognized along the valley of the River Tonge and Eagley Brook. Here, the residential function is almost absent. In the nineteenth century, factories were usually set in the midst of houses, whereas newer factories tend to be built in open spaces. The factory labelled A in fig. 6 has recently been built well away from residential areas on what was formerly a large area of playing fields. There is no longer the need for people to live near the industry in which they work, because they no longer have to walk to work.

The central area of a town, usually the original nucleus, tends to take on a different character from the rest of the town. As the town expands, this area loses most of its former residents and industrial premises, and becomes devoted almost exclusively to

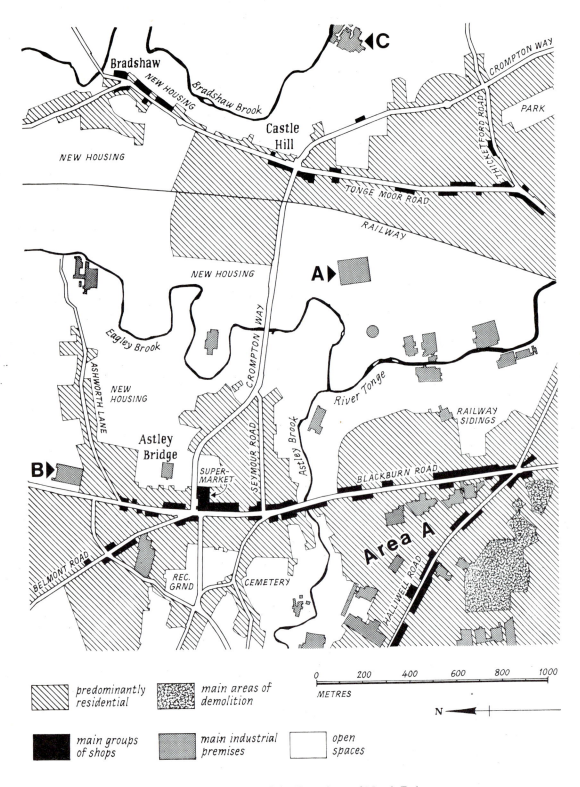

Fig. 6   The Pattern of the Functions of North Bolton

shops, offices, entertainment, hotels and public service and administration. Because of the predominance of these functions, the central area has been called the Central Business District (C.B.D.). Most of its few residents tend to live in flats above shops or offices and industrial concerns are usually in fairly small premises in back streets. Within the central area it may even be possible to distinguish separate areas devoted largely to offices, public administration, entertainment, or particular types of shops.

Outside the central area, there may be smaller business districts consisting of smaller concentrations of shops and offices. These are referred to as suburban service centres.

From this brief account it can be seen that the morphology of a town may be very complicated indeed. On the pattern of ages and types of buildings created by the growth of the town (fig. 3), there is superimposed the pattern of the functions of the town (fig. 6). There may be old and new suburban service centres, old and new high-class residential areas, old and new industrial zones, etc. By urban field work we are able to recognize these complex geographical patterns.

Using the above material, try to answer the questions at the end of this chapter.

Suggested Plan

To make a field study of the morphology of a whole town or a large part of a town, the most useful Ordnance Survey map to use is on a scale of 1 : 2500 (25·344 inches to 1 mile). At this scale, except in the centres of some ancient towns, the spaces representing in- dividual buildings are large enough to contain a symbol written in the field. Also, on this scale, a considerable area of a town is represented on one Ordnance Survey sheet.

One difficulty is that Ordnance Survey maps can never be completely up to date. Hence, it is necessary when in the field to sketch in the outlines of the areas of building which have been completed since the town was last surveyed. Many of the Ordnance Survey maps which are still available were published in the 1950s. In some isolated districts, the most recent Ordnance Survey map may date back to the early part of this century. Hence, later buildings have to be drawn in. This may be inconvenient during field work, but the end product provides a ready-made indication on the completed map of recent extensions of the settlement pattern.

In studying urban morphology, as many as possible of the town's functions must be recorded in the field. It is necessary to walk through the town marking the field symbols on every building shown on the map. In the classroom afterwards, the field symbols are changed into a system of colours and symbols to produce a clear pattern on the finished map.

a) Survey Instructions

The survey of the morphology of a town should concern itself with the recording of the use of every building at *ground floor level*. Upper floors may have different uses from the ground floor, but the recording of these introduces rather difficult mapping problems. On the whole it is better to restrict the study of upper floor functions to detailed surveys of small parts of the town, such as the central area or particular streets.

The morphology of a town should be surveyed under the following headings:

i) Residence
The aim here is to record both the ages and the types of houses. In any particular town

it will be possible to recognize and to map a great many different types and ages of houses. The number of possible house types will be different in every district. The following general survey method can be applied to any town.

(a) As a broad general rule, most terraced houses were built before and most semi-detached houses were built after World War I. In the survey, pre-World War I houses are given the symbol **P** and post-World War I houses are given the symbol **M**.

(b) Different sizes and types of houses in each age group may be distinguished. There is of course an enormous variety of possible sizes and types, but it is usually possible to recognize three major types of house in each of the two age groups.

Pre-World War I houses (**P**) may be subdivided into small terraced types (**P1**), larger terraced or semi-detached (**P2**) and large detached houses set in their own fairly extensive grounds (**P3**). In any particular town, the surveyor should decide for himself how he will distinguish between these three types. Sometimes, for instance, a **P2** house can be distinguished from a **P1** by the fact that it possesses a large bay window or a fairly ornate front door. These details have to be decided in relation to the particular town which is being surveyed.

Post-World War I houses are more easily classified into council houses (**M1**), privately owned houses of small or medium size and price (**M2**), and privately owned large or expensive houses (**M3**). The **M2** type are usually semi-detached or small detached houses and bungalows, but they may be terraced. The **M3** type are usually large detached or semi-detached houses and bungalows, and are usually found in a variety of different styles in the same street.

A building should be classified in the 'Residence' category if the ground floor of the street frontage is used as a residence. Groups of garages for private cars should be classified as 'Residence' and should be labelled **Garages**. Residential hotels should be labelled **H** unless the town is a holiday resort (see 'Resort Function' on page 21).

ii) Industry

The types of industries carried on in all industrial premises should be recorded. The ground floor of a building used for industry should be given the symbol **I**. A number is added to this symbol to indicate the general type of industry, and the actual name of the type of industry should be recorded if possible. A useful classification of industries is shown below:

I1 Industries which are generally concerned with the processing of raw materials which are mined or quarried. These include such industries as metal working, engineering of all kinds and the manufacture of chemicals, glass, pottery, cement and similar products.

I2 The manufacture of textiles, leather goods and clothing.

I3 The processing of food and drink products and tobacco.

I4 Printing and the manufacture of wood and paper.

I5 Service industries. This category includes all non-manufacturing industries and is mainly connected with public utilities, transport and storage. It includes bus and waterworks depots, dairies, coal distributing firms, timber yards, warehouses of all kinds, gas and electricity works. It is important not to confuse this type of industry with shops. A useful guide to remember is that wholesale distribution (distribution of goods to shops) is classified under service industry, but retail distribution (sale of goods to the public) is classified under shops. A service garage which provides repair facilities for cars is classified as a service industry, but a petrol station which provides no repair facilities is classified as a shop.

iii) Shops

All shops situated on the ground floor of the street frontage are allocated the general symbol **S**. In making a survey of a whole town or a large part of a town it is better not to subdivide the shops into more detailed categories. This may be done in more detailed studies of the central area or suburban service centres. A shop is broadly defined as a place where a member of the public may buy a commodity or obtain a service. Shops include the usual food, clothing and household goods shops, together with cafés, snack bars, fish and chip shops, betting shops, hairdressers, launderettes, gas, electricity and motor car showrooms. Petrol stations with no car repair facilities are also shops. A full list of shop types is provided on page 46.

iv) Offices

Offices are given the general symbol **O**. Again, to qualify for inclusion in this type of survey the office must occupy the ground floor street frontage of a building. Many offices are located above shops in the centre of a town. These may be plotted in more detailed surveys of small areas of towns. In a survey of a whole town or a large part of a town it is again better not to subdivide offices into their various types. There are a large number of different types of offices, including professional offices (e.g. solicitors), financial offices (e.g. insurance companies), trade offices (offices of industrial undertakings), transport offices and political and government offices (e.g. trade unions, inland revenue, etc.). It is useful to distinguish

banks (**Bank**) and doctors' (**Doc**) and dentists' (**Dent**) surgeries.

v) Entertainment

This category is given the general symbol **E** and consists of the ground floors of premises which people visit for purposes of entertainment. In addition to obvious entertainment facilities such as cinemas, theatres, bowling alleys, dance halls and bingo halls, it also includes public houses, social clubs of various kinds and slot machine arcades. Public assembly halls which are used for a variety of purposes such as concerts, shows, conferences, etc. should be classified as public buildings (see below). Cinemas and theatres (**EC**), dance halls (**ED**) and public houses (**EP**) should be distinguished by symbols, as shown, but in all other cases, the actual type of entertainment should be labelled in full.

vi) Public Buildings

This category consists of buildings used by the public which are owned and organized by public authorities. It includes public libraries and museums, swimming baths, clinics, schools, churches, public assembly halls (see above), hospitals, etc. The use of the building should be labelled in full.

vii) Open Spaces

The name of the use of the land should be labelled on the map. For example playing fields, car parks, cemeteries, parks, bowling greens, allotment gardens, wasteland, etc. should be indicated.

viii) Resort Function

If the town being surveyed is a holiday resort the symbol **H** for a residential hotel should be omitted and replaced by a general symbol **R** together with a number indicating the type of hotel. It is difficult to produce a classification of hotels which works successfully in all holiday resorts. The following schemes have been found to be useful in particular resorts:

R1 Small boarding house with not more than two windows on the ground floor street frontage.

R2 Larger boarding house or hotel which is part of a terraced block.

R3 Large hotel, either detached or semi-detached.

or:

R1 Unlicensed hotel or boarding house.

R2 Licensed hotel with only a drive or a small car park.

R3 Licensed hotel with a large car park.

ix) Derelict Land and Property

Very often large and small areas of towns are in the process of being cleared for redevelopment (urban renewal). This process should be recorded. It is useful to indicate when a building shown on the Ordnance Survey map has been demolished (**DEM**) and in some cases the shape of the replacement building may be sketched on the map. Buildings which have not been demolished but which are permanently out of use and obviously decaying should be shown by the symbol **DER** (Derelict). Vacant shops and industrial premises which appear likely to be reoccupied at some future date should be classified as shops and industrial buildings.

---

b) Summary of Survey Scheme for Use in the Field

Record only the uses of the *ground floors* of buildings.

Major Category of Land Use

i) Residence

Mark the symbols shown both in the field and on the final map. Do not colour the final map.

Subdivisions of the Major Category

Outline the areas of each of the following categories and label with the symbols indicated.

P1 Small, terraced, pre-World War I housing.

P2 Larger, terraced or semi-detached, pre-World War I housing.

P3 Large, pre-World War I houses set in their own large grounds.

M1 Modern council housing.

M2 Modern, privately owned housing of small or medium size and price.

M3 Modern large or expensive detached or semi-detached houses.

H Residential hotel (not to be used in holiday resort).

ii) Industry

Mark **I** in the field.
Colour Red on the final map.

Subdivide by adding a number to the general field symbol **I**. This number should also be printed over the red colour on the final map.

I1 Metal working, engineering, chemicals, glass, pottery, cement, etc.
I2 Textiles, leather goods, clothing.
I3 Food, drink, tobacco.
I4 Printing, manufacture of wood and paper.
I5 Service industries.
Any other industry – label **I**.
In all cases, label the *name* of the industry if possible.

iii) Shops

Mark **S** in the field.
Colour Yellow on the final map.

Do not subdivide shops.
Label **Petrol Station** and **Supermarket** by name.

iv) Offices

Mark **O** in the field.
Colour Blue on the final map.

Do not subdivide offices. Label **Bank**, doctor's surgery (**Doc**), dentist's surgery (**Dent**).

v) Entertainment

Mark **E** in the field.
Colour Orange on the final map.

Subdivide by adding a letter to the general field symbol **E**. This letter should also be printed over the orange colour on the final map.
EC Cinemas and theatres.
ED Dance halls.
EP Public houses (not residential).
In all other cases, label the *name* of the type of entertainment.

vi) Public Buildings

Mark the name in full both in the field and on the final map.
Colour Green on the final map.

No subdivision necessary.

vii) Open Spaces

Mark the *name* of their function in full both in the field and on the final map.
Do not colour the final map.

No subdivision necessary.

viii) Resort Function

Mark **R** in the field.
Colour Purple on the final map.

Omit the symbol **H** under 'Residence'.
Subdivide by adding a number to the

general field symbol **R**. This number should be printed over the purple colour on the final map.

EITHER:
R1 Small boarding house with not more than two windows on the ground floor street frontage.
R2 Larger boarding house or hotel which is part of a terraced block.
R3 Large hotel, either detached or semi-detached.
OR:
R1 Unlicensed hotel or boarding house.
R2 Licensed hotel with only a drive or a small car park.
R3 Licensed hotel with a large car park.

xi) Derelict Land and Property
Mark the symbols given across both in the field and on the final map.
Do not colour the final map.

Outline the areas of each of the following categories and label with the symbols indicated.
DEM Building demolished. Insert the new use of the land if possible.
DER Building still standing but out of use and decaying.

Exercises
Refer to figs. 3 and 6.
1   Name or state the locations of three hamlets existing in 1845 which were: (a) at road junctions, (b) on the sides of the deeply incised river valleys.

2   At what approximate dates did the northward expansion of Bolton reach (a) Astley Bridge, (b) Castle Hill?

3   In a town it is common to find older houses situated along a road frontage and newer houses to the rear of them. It indicates that settlement initially occurred in the form of ribbon development along the road and then the land to the rear was filled in by later settlement. Name two roads which show this pattern of settlement.

4   Suggest a reason why there has been little building on the east side of Tonge Moor Road, north of Castle Hill.

5   What evidence is there on the map that Crompton Way is a recently built road?

6 State three different factors which seem to have influenced the settlement pattern in the area between the River Tonge-Eagley Brook and Bradshaw Brook (see fig. 6).

7 Suggest a reason why early industrial development took place along the river valleys. Why could later developments move away from the valleys?

8 Suggest a reason why there are fewer shops in the Tonge Moor Road area than along Blackburn Road.

9 Groups of shops tend to be concentrated near road junctions. Describe the locations of five examples.

10 In which shopping areas would you expect trade to increase in the future?

11 Industrial premises occupy two contrasting types of locations. Describe these and state the locations of examples.

12 Why do you think that there are no shops on Crompton Way between the supermarket at Astley Bridge and the Castle Hill road junction? (See figs. 3 and 6.)

13 At what approximate dates were the following built:
a) the houses which are being demolished to the south-west of Halliwell Road?
b) the mills in the angle between Halliwell Road and Blackburn Road (area A)?
c) the mill on the east side of Blackburn Road in the far north (B)?
d) the mill on Bradshaw Brook (C)? (See fig. 6.)

14 Describe the locations of:
a) three separate areas of modern buildings with little or no industry,
b) two areas of nineteenth century housing closely associated with industrial development.

15 Why is there no demolition in the Tonge Moor Road area?

16 Draw a simplified sketch map of north Bolton using information from figs. 3 and 6. First of all draw the railway and the main pattern of roads and rivers. Then sketch the approximate areas of the following types of urban regions:
a) major shopping areas,
b) valley industrial zones,
c) areas of mixed functions (nineteenth century housing and industry),
d) nineteenth century housing with little industry,
e) twentieth century residential areas.

3 Examples of the Field Study of Urban Morphology

This chapter contains brief studies of the urban morphology of three contrasting types of towns. Astley Bridge is a part of Bolton in which industry and residential settlement developed rapidly in the latter half of the nineteenth century. During the twentieth century industry has tended to decline in importance but modern residential areas have been added to the settlement pattern. Poole is an ancient port, with a long tradition of maritime trade, which is adapting itself to modern conditions of industry and commerce. Torquay is predominantly a holiday resort but it also fulfils important service functions. Its urban morphology has been influenced strongly by relief features.

Astley Bridge

The three major processes involved in making a study of urban morphology are illustrated in figs. 7a, b and c. The area selected is Astley Bridge, a part of north Bolton whose growth has already been described with the aid of old maps (figs. 2 a, b and c, page 6). The survey area extends along Blackburn Road between the early clusters of settlement at Hills Fold in the north and Astley Bridge in the south

(fig. 2a) and eastwards to include part of the modern Crompton Way. Astley Bridge illustrates over a hundred years of urban growth.

a) The Field Survey (fig. 7a)

The actual field work has been carried out by using the scheme explained in the previous chapter and an Ordnance Survey map of 1 : 2500 scale.

i) Residence

Over the last hundred years or so a great many different types of houses have been built in Astley Bridge. In particular there is a wide range of pre-World War I houses. In the survey it is easy to allocate the rows of small terraced houses, as found in Sherwood Street and Wilton Street in the south, to the **P1** category. It is also easy to recognize the large detached house, Linwood (Seymour Road), as a **P3** type. Between these two extremes there is a great variety of types. It has been decided to allocate the category **P2** to terraced houses possessing bay windows and larger houses in pairs or in groups of three. This means that the **P2** category includes a considerable range of house types, but a more detailed classification would be too clumsy to include in a general morphological survey. The modern houses present no

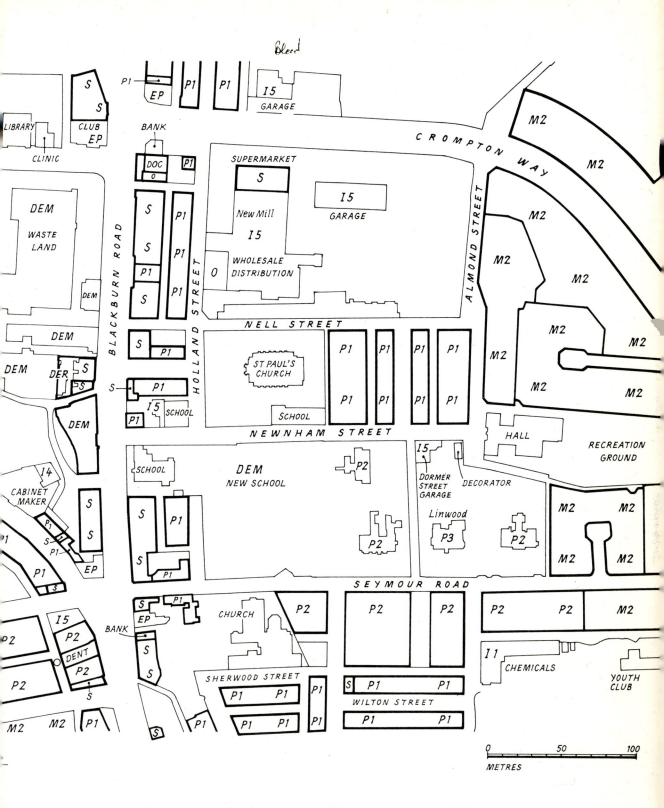

Fig. 7a A Map Compiled during a Field Study of Astley Bridge

problem. Most of the houses are found in uni-form groups. This facilitates field work be-cause it is possible to draw a line round a group of houses and mark a symbol for the whole group instead of having to record each house individually. This can be seen in the case of the four blocks of **P1** houses to the east of St. Paul's Church (fig. 7a).

ii) Industry

The cotton industry has now disappeared from the area shown on the map. The large cotton mill to the west of Blackburn Road has been completely demolished, hence this area has been labelled **DEM**. No new development has yet taken place on this land. New Mill, to the east of Blackburn Road, has been partially demolished, but other parts have been adapted for use as a supermarket and a warehouse and office concerned with the wholesale distribution of groceries. The approximate outline of the supermarket has been sketched in on fig. 7a.

iii) Shops

Shops present few mapping problems. Since most of them occur along Blackburn Road, it is possible to outline groups of shops, thus making recording easy. A small group of vacant shops on the west side of Blackburn Road have been labelled **DER** because they are in such a poor condition that they appear unlikely to be reoccupied. The approximate outline of a modern petrol station and service garage on the south side of Crompton Way has been sketched in.

iv) Offices

Most of the offices occupy adapted houses and could easily be overlooked. It is impor-tant in a field survey that *every* building should be examined carefully.

v) Public Buildings

The complicated outline of the new school on the cleared land between Newnham Street and Seymour Road could not be drawn accurately in the field, so its location has simply been labelled (fig. 7a).

b) The Production of the Final Map (fig. 7b).

On this map, residential, demolished and derelict property are neatly labelled in exactly the same way as in the field. Industry, shops, offices and public buildings are given their relevant colours instead of their field symbols, the different types of industries being distinguished by their *index numbers only*. Wherever possible, the actual uses of industrial buildings, offices, public build-ings and open spaces, are written in full.

c) The Map of Urban Zones (fig. 7c)

A careful study of fig. 7b reveals that parti-cular urban functions are generally located in particular areas. For example, it is easy to see at a glance that shops are arranged in a strip along Blackburn Road and that modern housing is grouped in a solid block on each side of Crompton Way. By placing a piece of tracing paper over fig. 7b it is easy to distinguish and outline certain areas which are given over to particular urban functions. The result is a diagram showing the broad pattern of urban morphology in Astley Bridge (fig. 7c).

One can easily distinguish the following elements in the urban pattern:

1. A linear strip of shops and offices along Blackburn Road, especially on the east side.

2. A strip of **P1** housing immediately to the east of this shopping strip.

3. A strip of **P2/P3** housing along Seymour Road with **P1** housing to the rear on the north and south sides.

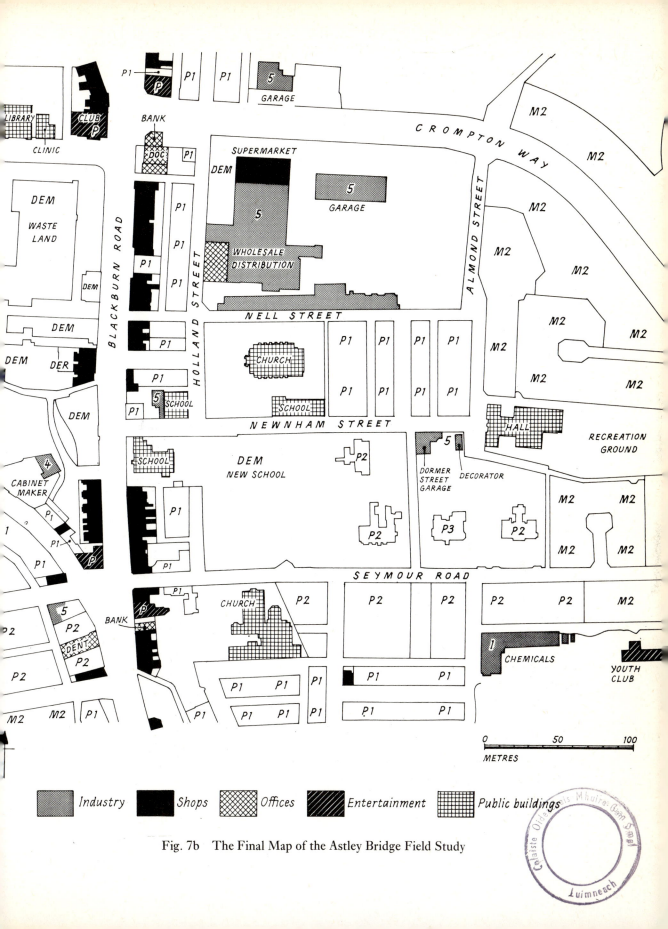

Fig. 7b   The Final Map of the Astley Bridge Field Study

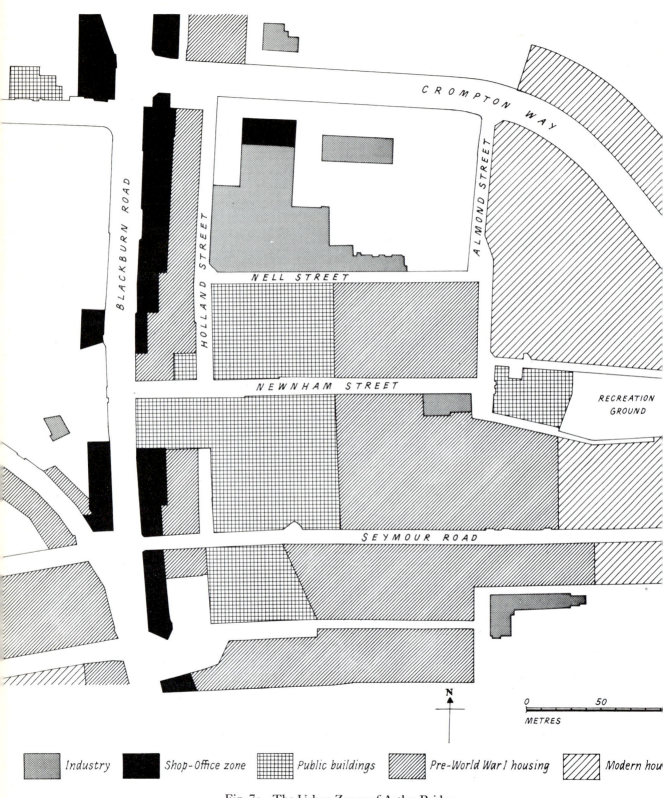

CROMPTON WAY

BLACKBURN ROAD

HOLLAND STREET

ALMOND STREET

NELL STREET

NEWNHAM STREET

SEYMOUR ROAD

RECREATION GROUND

N

0   50
METRES

| | Industry | | Shop-Office zone | | Public buildings | | Pre-World War I housing | | Modern hou |

Fig. 7c   The Urban Zones of Astley Bridge

4. Large areas among the **P** type housing devoted to churches and schools. Some of these were built in the nineteenth century at about the same time as the houses; others were built in the twentieth century on land freed by the demolition of nineteenth century buildings.

5. Industries have a scattered distribution and often occupy buildings which formerly had other uses (e.g. New Mill, Dormer Street Garage).

6. **M** type housing is found almost exclusively in the east and consists almost entirely of semi-detached houses, some in planned estates and others as ribbon development along Crompton Way.

7. The two banks and the doctor's and the dentist's surgeries are situated in the shopping belt along Blackburn Road.

The field survey reveals that Astley Bridge is a predominantly residential area which possesses a small shopping area, probably concerned with providing for the day to day needs of the local residents.

d) Suggested Follow-up Work

In the course of carrying out a field study of urban morphology a great many ideas will suggest themselves for further study both in the field and in the library or classroom. These follow-up studies will add to one's understanding of the urban area.

1. In Astley Bridge a great variety of different house types have been built since the middle of the nineteenth century. These could be sketched, dated and arranged in an approximate chronological order to illustrate changing architectural styles and details of the growth of the town.

2. Details of the types of shops found in the linear shopping belt could be discovered. This aspect is dealt with later in the section on suburban service centres.

3. There appear to be few large employers of labour among the industries of Astley Bridge, and the considerable number of modern semi-detached houses suggests a commuting population. The extent to which people move out of the area to work, and where they actually work, could be investigated.

4. The library may possess copies of commercial directories for the study area which were published many years ago. These directories give the names, addresses and occupations of householders by streets, and also names and addresses of industrial undertakings and the type of industry. In Astley Bridge's case, directories are available for selected years since the 1840s. From these, it is possible to map the distribution of shops and industries and to some extent residential property, thus building up a map of the urban morphology of perhaps eighty years ago. It is interesting to compare this with the present-day map.

5. The supermarket on Crompton Way looks rather too large to serve the needs of the population of Astley Bridge alone. It would be interesting to try to map the area from which customers travel to shop here. Similarly, the catchment areas for the library, the Club, the Youth Club, the churches and the schools could be investigated. This would reveal something of Astley Bridge's links with the surrounding area.

6. The centre of Bolton lies just over one and a half kilometres to the south along Blackburn Road; Crompton Way is the northern by-pass around the centre of Bolton. A great deal of the traffic along these roads passes straight through Astley Bridge. It would be interesting to count the numbers of private and commercial vehicles passing along Blackburn Road and Crompton Way and to try to account for the patterns of traffic flow.

7. Visits might be arranged to the various industrial undertakings and questions asked along the lines suggested on pages 10 and 11.

Nearly all towns lend themselves to this type of study. A collection of maps, notes, drawings and diagrams made up in the ways suggested above constitutes a very worth-while geographical study of a town. Much additional knowledge will be gained even about a town which is familiar.

Poole

a) Background Information

The older part of the town of Poole is situated on a small peninsula between Holes Bay and Parkstone Bay on the north side of Poole Harbour, in Dorset. Here is the ancient port of Poole. In more modern times the town has expanded northwards and eastwards to link up with the westward expansion of Bournemouth, thus creating a small conurbation.

The southern and western (Holes Bay) sides of the peninsula are lined with quays (fig. 8) and a railway line crosses the neck of the peninsula to the north. Road access to this part of Poole is restricted in several ways. One main road approaches from the north-east and divides into West Quay Road and High Street, which both cross the railway at level crossings (fig. 8). A close network of roads and streets covers the peninsula, but many of these, as may be expected in this ancient part of the town, are very narrow and winding. Road access to the peninsula from the south is via Poole Bridge which spans Little Channel between Poole and Lower Hamworthy.

The evidence of several centuries of urban evolution is found in the townscape of peninsular Poole. Old, picturesque buildings and irregular street patterns contrast strongly with modern industrial developments.

Poole has a population of over 90 000. The peninsula is only a part of the total urban area.

b) Summary of the Field Work Results (fig. 8)

i) Residence

Residential areas are found to the east and west of High Street. The old residential part of the town lies to the west of High Street. Here houses of a wide variety of architectural styles – sometimes stone, sometimes brick – are set in a complicated pattern of narrow, winding streets and are often closely grouped together with industrial undertakings. Many of these buildings are extremely picturesque, but a large-scale clearance programme is completely changing the urban scene. As old property is demolished the cleared sites are used temporarily as car parks. New, wider streets, driven across the cleared sites, are replacing the old street pattern.

To the east of High Street, urban renewal has proceeded more quickly. Much older housing has been demolished and the sites have been redeveloped for council housing or high blocks of council flats. Surviving P type houses are usually of the brick-built 'industrial' type.

ii) Industry

Industrial development contributes a very clear pattern to the town's morphology. Industrial areas form an almost complete ring round the peninsula, extending along West Quay in the west, The Quay in the south and the railway in the north. In addition, smaller industrial undertakings are scattered through the residential areas.

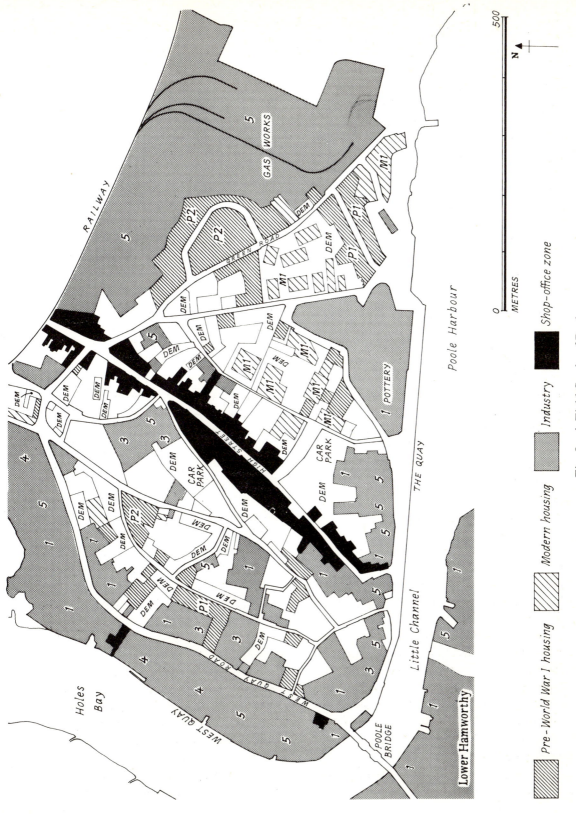

GAS WORKS

RAILWAY

P2
P2
M1
P1
P1
M1
DEM
GREEN ROAD
DEM
DEM
M1
DEM
DEM
DEM
DEM
DEM
DEM
M1
M1
DEM
DEM
M1
M1
5
DEM
M1
DEM
5
DEM
DEM
5
DEM
M1
POTTERY
1
DEM
DEM
DEM
DEM
CAR PARK
DEM
DEM
CAR PARK
4
HIGH STREET
DEM
DEM
5
3
3
DEM
5
DEM
DEM
DEM
5
P2
DEM
DEM
DEM
5
1
DEM
DEM
DEM
5
1
1
DEM
1
5
1
5
5
1
5
DEM
1
3
P1
DEM
5
3
DEM
5
5
1
5
THE QUAY
1
1

Poole Harbour

Holes Bay

WEST QUAY

WEST QUAY ROAD

4
4
5
5
1
1
3
1
5
5
1
1
1
POOLE BRIDGE
1
Little Channel
5
5
1

Lower Hamworthy

N

0   METRES   500

Pre-World War I housing
Modern housing
Industry
Shop-office zone

Fig. 8   A Field Study of Poole

Near the West Quay, engineering and chemical firms (1) and timber yards (4) are particularly prominent. Similarly, on the Lower Hamworthy side of Little Channel there is a stress on engineering (1) including shipbuilding. In contrast, along The Quay in the south, the emphasis is on service industry (5) in the form of warehouses which are occupied in handling the general trade of the port. Road access to the rear of these warehouses is particularly difficult because of the narrow, winding streets. East of Green Road is the gas works.

iii) Shops and Offices

There is a very simple pattern of shops and offices, extending across the peninsula from north-east to south-west along each side of High Street.

In peninsular Poole, therefore, field work reveals that the major urban functions separate out quite clearly and produce a remarkably symmetrical pattern of urban zones. Change in the townscape is very rapid as the old port adapts itself to modern conditions.

Torquay

a) Background Information

The Torquay peninsula is a dissected plateau composed largely of Devonian limestone. River erosion in the past has excavated a number of deep, narrow valleys. Remnants of the former plateau surface make up the eight hills over which the town of Torquay has been built. The Devonian limestone forms steep, often precipitous, valley sides.

The survey area (fig. 9) is situated on the south side of the Torquay peninsula im-

mediately inland from the harbour. It is a narrow valley running approximately from north to south across the area, flanked by hills rising to about sixty metres. Valleyside slopes are everywhere steep and often precipitous (fig. 9). The average gradient from Fleet Street to Warren Road is about 1 in 4, and from Abbey Place to Warren Road about 1 in 2·5. Warren Hill rises twelve metres in a distance of just over seventy metres. Prominent cliff-like outcrops of limestone run along the steep valley sides.

Relief features have exerted a strong influence on the street pattern. Fleet Street follows the valley floor and rises slowly from about three and a half metres at the Strand to about nine metres near the General Post Office. Most other streets run roughly parallel to Fleet Street. By doing this they either follow the contours and remain fairly level or they cut obliquely across the steep slopes, so gaining height gradually. The acute angles formed by the junctions of Braddons Hill Road West and The Terrace illustrate this feature. It is interesting to trace the possible route for a vehicle from the point marked X (fig. 9) to Warren Road. Footpaths for pedestrians tend to run at right-angles to the streets, and height is gained quickly by means of flights of stone steps. The summits of the hills are fairly level.

b) Summary of the Field Work Results
(fig. 9)

i) Residence

Residential property occupies the slopes and summits of the hills to the east and west of Fleet Street. Most houses are of the **P** type, built before World War I. A fairly clear division is seen, particularly to the west of Fleet Street, between **P1** and **P2** houses occupying less desirable positions on the

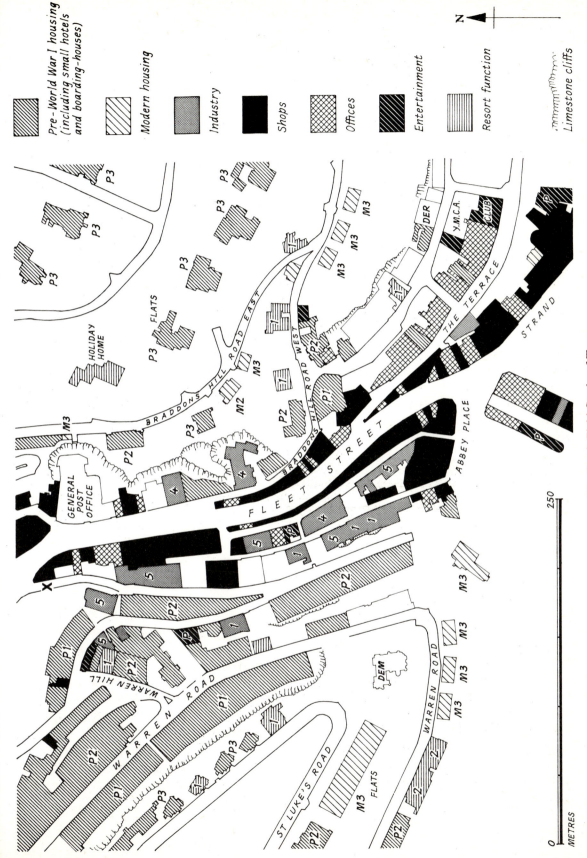

Key:

Pre-World War I housing (including small hotels and boarding-houses)

Modern housing

Industry

Shops

Offices

Entertainment

Resort function

Limestone cliffs

N

Fig. 9   A Field Study of Torquay

0   METRES   250

GENERAL POST OFFICE

HOLIDAY HOME

BRADDONS HILL ROAD EAST

BRADDONS HILL ROAD WEST

FLEET STREET

WARREN HILL

WARREN ROAD

ST LUKE'S ROAD

WARREN ROAD

ABBEY PLACE

THE TERRACE

STRAND

Y.M.C.A.

CLUB

DER

DEM

FLATS

FLATS

X

P1   P2   P3   M2   M3

valley sides, below the level of the limestone cliffs, and **P3** houses built on the gently sloping hill summits, commanding extensive views across Tor Bay. The **P1** houses in long terraces along Warren Road, for example, are immediately backed by a precipitous slope and face north-eastwards, away from Tor Bay. In some cases the **P3** houses on the summits have been converted into hotels and flats. Relatively few houses have been built in this area since World War I. These are mostly expensive **M3** residences situated in favoured elevated positions overlooking Tor Bay. Others are in the form of blocks of expensive, privately owned flats, also occupying elevated positions.

A striking contrast in settlement patterns is observed. Below the level of the limestone cliffs, closely packed terraces of **P1** and **P2** houses are aligned along the hillsides and the parallel roads. On the summits, above the limestone cliffs, detached residences are set between wide, tree-lined avenues. The limestone cliffs form a clear demarcation line between these contrasting settlement patterns.

ii) Industry

Industrial undertakings are distributed along the valley floor to the rear of the Fleet Street frontage. These are mainly warehouses (5), small engineering workshops (1), service garages (5) and printing works (4), including that of the local newspaper. It is interesting to note that the cliff line appears to determine the shape of the printing works (4) to the east of Fleet Street.

iii) Shops

Shops are almost restricted to a narrow strip along each side of Fleet Street, widening somewhat in the south at Abbey Place and the Strand, where there is a large department store. Fleet Street is clearly the main axis of movement so that shops derive an advantage from a street frontage location. Such a location is not so important for industry.

iv) Offices

Those offices which may derive advantage from prominent sites in the major shopping area, where many pedestrians are moving, are distributed along the shopping strip of Fleet Street, with a particular concentration at its lower end near the Strand. They are mostly banks and the offices of insurance companies, estate agents and building societies. A distinct office zone is found along The Terrace, where solicitors, accountants, insurance companies and estate agents occupy large **P2** type terraced houses.

v) Resort Function

There is no special concentration of hotels. Most are scattered haphazardly among the **P3** and **M3** houses of the hill summits and also in the terraces of the west side of the valley, particularly along Warren Road. Most of the hotels of this part of Torquay are of a moderate size and unlicensed (1).

The Fleet Street area of Torquay shows a clear pattern of urban zones which is related closely to the strong relief features of the area. A transect westwards from Fleet Street passes through the full range of urban zones, from shops along the main street frontage to industry to their rear, **P1/P2** housing on the valley side, and finally **P3/M3** housing and hotels on the hill summit. Moving eastwards from Fleet Street, there is less space before the limestone cliff is reached, so the industrial zone reaches the cliff and the **P1/P2** houses are usually absent (fig. 9).

Exercises

1 Make tracings of the street plans shown on fig. 8 (Poole) and fig. 9 (Torquay). Construct maps showing the broad urban zones which may be recognized in these areas. The following major zones should be recognized and outlined:

a) Poole: (i) shopping/office zone, (ii) industrial zone, (iii) zone of mixed functions (including old residential, demolition and industrial), (iv) residential zone, (v) redeveloped residential zone.

b) Torquay: (i)shopping zone, (ii) office zone, (iii) industrial zone, (iv) old residential zone (smaller houses) (v) residential (large houses)/resort zone.

NOTE: The drawing of a map of urban zones involves a certain amount of personal judgement. The aim should be to produce a clear pattern as shown in fig. 7c.

2 Every town is different from every other town, but it may be possible to recognize broad similarities in certain respects. Make a comparison between Astley Bridge, Poole and Torquay by comparing either fig. 7b (Astley Bridge) with fig. 8 (Poole) and fig. 9 (Torquay), or fig. 7c with your own urban zones maps of Poole and Torquay.

a) Make a list of similarities in the urban morphology of the three areas. Consider the following points: (i) the shapes of the shopping zones, (ii) the distribution of industrial property, (iii) the types of residential property, (iv) the relationship of residential areas to shopping and industrial zones. Give a brief explanation of why you think these similarities exist.

b) Make a list of the ways in which each area differs from the other two areas. In the case of each area, give a brief explanation of why you think it is different from the other two.

3 By reference to fig. 8, study the transport facilities which exist in peninsular Poole. What advantages of transport does the area possess? What disadvantages may there be? In what ways does transport seem to have an influence on the pattern of urban land use?

4 Using examples from your own town or from any other town you know discuss the problems of the conflict between the traditionalists, who wish to preserve historically interesting buildings, and the progressives who think that the functional efficiency of a town is of primary importance.

5 From the information about Torquay provided in this chapter, draw an approximate section to show the rise and fall of the land along a line running from St. Luke's Road in the west to Braddons Hill Road East in the east. Mark on the section the different uses of the land.

6 a) Make a list of questions which could be asked to improve one's knowledge of the urban geography of Poole if one visited (i) a pottery on The Quay, (ii) a timber yard, (iii) a shipbuilding yard, (iv) a local government official.

   b) Set out programmes in as much detail as possible for follow-up studies which might be undertaken in the field and in the library or classroom to increase one's knowledge of the urban geography of Poole and Torquay.

4 The Field Study of the Central Area of a Town

General Principles

a) Characteristics of the Central Area

The central area of the town is the main part of the town in which goods and services are exchanged between buyers and sellers. People travel to the central area from other parts of the town and from outside the town to avail themselves of the facilities it provides for shopping, entertainment, and professional, educational, cultural and other services. Hence, the central area is said to possess the quality of centrality. This does not mean that it is necessarily the geometrical centre of the town; it is central in terms of movement and influence. London, for example, has a higher degree of centrality than any other city in Britain, but it is not geometrically central within Britain.

A place which possesses centrality may be termed a 'central place'. People travel to it to satisfy certain wants. One of the simplest types of central place is the grouping of a church, an inn, a primary school and a general shop in a village. Various groups of people travel at various times from other parts of the village and from the surrounding countryside to use these services. Similarly, small corner shops, usually grocer/off-licences, in towns, are small central places. The greatest concentration of services in a town, and therefore the place which possesses the highest degree of centrality, is known as the central area of the town, or sometimes as the Central Business District.

The central area is usually located somewhere near the old nucleus of the town, usually where most roads converge. In former times this area would be used for residence. As trade grew, service activities developed, and these tended to cluster together because they derived advantages through being close to one another. In the central area of a modern town it is obvious that different services help one another. For example, there is a clear advantage to be gained by the market, the shops, the restaurants, the bus station and the car parks being close to one another. Car parks near shops and markets make shopping expeditions more convenient. Restaurants gain trade by providing facilities for tired shoppers. Similarly, advantages are to be gained by banks being located near shops, theatres near car parks and hotels near railway stations. Because of these benefits, service functions of many kinds have become concentrated in the central areas of towns. These services exist to serve the needs of both the whole urban community and, in most cases, a surrounding area containing smaller towns and villages.

As services have become concentrated in central areas, the resident population has moved out. Now it is rather rare to find people living in the central area. As towns have grown, the population of their central areas has decreased. Probably only about three hundred of Bolton's approximate population of 150 000 live in its central area. As a result, many journeys have to be made to and from central areas. The central area is very densely populated during the day when it is occupied by shoppers and office and shop workers, but it is almost empty by night. The morning and evening 'rush hours', inward and outward 'tidal' flows, are characteristic features of life in larger towns.

Similarly, industries of various kinds, established long ago in the central part of the town, may find that they have little room to expand, or may encounter difficult transport problems. Firms may then decide to move to the outskirts. The cattle market and various shoe firms in Norwich have moved outwards in this way. Industries which remain in the central area are usually those which derive a distinct advantage from a central location (e.g. warehousing), or from proximity to customers (e.g. printing) or because they are able to continue to work successfully in small, cramped premises.

There seems now to be a tendency for shops to move away from central areas. With increasing traffic congestion in central areas, and the expansion of residential suburbs, retail distributing firms are tending to build supermarkets and to occupy new shopping precincts near the outskirts of towns, where road access is easier.

b) The Form of the Central Area

In very small towns the central area may have a simple linear form along a single street. This has already been seen in the case of Astley Bridge (fig. 7b). Another example is Longridge (fig. 11), a small town (population: about 5 700) a few kilometres from Preston. A central area of this type may be difficult to define because its continuity is interrupted by residences along the street frontage, and there may be only a few other residences separating it from a separate, less important service area. This happens in the case of Longridge (fig. 11). Totnes (population: about 5 600) is another example of a town with a central area along a single street, though in this case the zone is more continuous. It is interesting to note that at Totnes the central area extends from the castle to the quay. These are two of the most important factors in the development of the town (fig. 10a). The single-street central area is sometimes varied by extensions along other streets. At Wareham, Dorset (population: about 3 500) the central area extends along three of the four main streets (fig. 10b). The central area of Horncastle, Lincolnshire (population: about 4 000) is mostly around the Market Place and High Street, but tongues do extend along the main roads leading out of the town (fig. 10c). Strangely enough, the central area of Poole (fig. 8) extends along a single street, although Poole has a population of over 90 000.

There is obviously a limit to the extent to which a central area can grow along a single street and still remain efficient, so larger examples tend to take on a more compact shape, spanning several streets. This can be seen in the case of Brixham (population: about 12 800) (fig. 12) and also in the case of Aberystwyth (population: about 10 200) (fig. 10e). In small holiday resorts it is common for the central area to extend from the railway station to the beach, both of which have been important factors encouraging urban growth. This can be seen clearly in the case of Skegness (fig. 10d) where Lumley Road is the main shopping thoroughfare, and also in the case of Aberystwyth (fig. 10e) where Terrace Road and Great Darkgate Street are the two main shopping arteries.

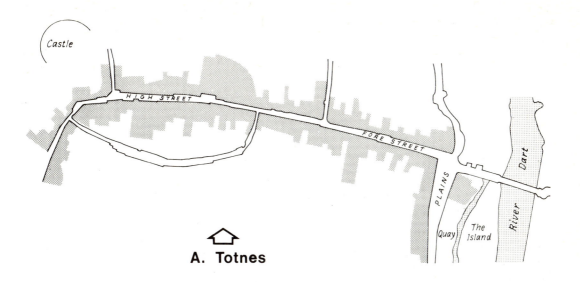

A. Totnes

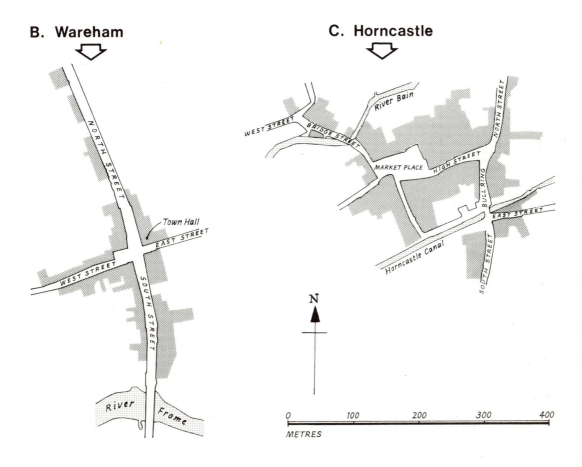

B. Wareham

C. Horncastle

Fig. 10   The Form of the Central Area of a) Totnes b) Wareham c) Horncastle

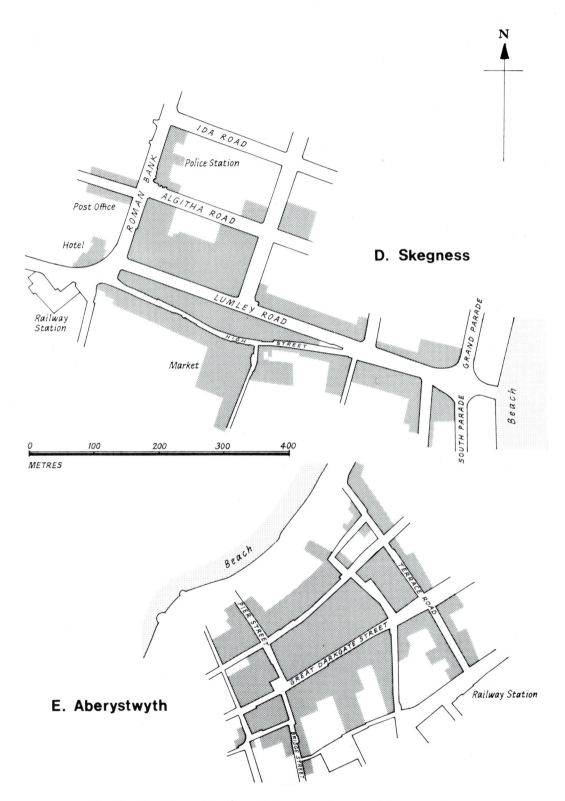

Fig. 10   The Form of the Central Area of d)Skegness e) Aberystwyth

Smaller central areas, such as the examples mentioned above, tend to consist of a rather haphazard mixture of shops, offices, entertainment facilities and small-scale industry. In many cases, however, shops exhibit a recognizable pattern in that they tend to occupy main street frontages with industrial premises located to their rear. In larger central areas, the different central area functions tend to occupy different parts of the central area. Thus it is possible to distinguish a distinct office zone, as in Torquay (fig. 9) and Bolton (fig. 13). In larger examples still, certain types of shops may concentrate in a particular part of the central area, and there may be recognizable zones of clothing shops or furniture shops.

The appearance of the central area is constantly changing; the process of urban renewal is almost continuous. Old buildings are demolished and new buildings appear; new glass or plastic fronts are fitted to older buildings. Hence it is impossible to trace any clear pattern of growth. On its fringes, the central area may expand into the surrounding residential zone. Often, large **P2** or **P3** type houses are taken over as office accommodation.

Roads and streets in the central area are crowded with traffic during the day, but because of strict parking regulations the car is difficult to use for movement within the central area. Most movement is on foot, and roads full of traffic passing through the town are serious barriers to pedestrian flow. Because of the road barriers pedestrians have to follow pavements, arcades and zebra crossings. The location of shops in relation to directions of pedestrian flows may be a significant factor influencing their trade. The modern idea is to separate the pedestrian from the vehicle completely, either by excluding vehicles entirely from the central area or by placing vehicles and pedestrians at different levels by means of subways or raised vehicle ramps. The principle of pedestrian-vehicle segregation has been employed in the designing of the central areas of New Towns and also in the redevelopment of the central areas of older towns such as Coventry.

The field study of a central area has much to contribute to the re-planning of the area.

c) The Status of the Central Area

Central areas differ in quality as well as in form. Each central area provides a different range of services. The variety and status of the services provided in any central area depend fundamentally on the spending power of the people who live in its trade area, that is, the area from which it draws buyers. This, in turn, depends upon the size of the trade area, the density of population, and the level of incomes within it.

It is well known that a village shop sells a wide variety of goods, including meat, vegetables, groceries, confectionery, sweets, simple household goods and sometimes clothes. A number of different retail trades are carried on under one roof. This is because the trade area of the village shop has insufficient spending power to support separate shops for the sale of each of these commodities. If housing estates are developed around a village, and its population increases, spending power will also increase, and the point may eventually be reached at which the village can support a separate confectioner's shop in addition to the general village shop. Spending power in the village is then said to have reached the 'threshold demand' for two shops instead of one. The term 'threshold demand' is used to indicate the smallest level of demand (spending power) which can support a particular establishment which provides a particular service. For example, one would not expect to find a branch of Woolworth's in a small village, because the threshold demand for a Woolworth's is above the actual level of demand (spending power) in the village. There is, in other words, too little spending power in the trade area of the village to support a branch of Woolworth's.

There are a great many threshold demands for different types of services. Services such as doctors, banks, food shops, household hardware shops and chemists have quite low thresholds, and therefore are often found in quite small central areas whose trade areas have low spending powers. On the other hand, the threshold demand for department stores, theatres, jewellers and national multiple shops selling furniture, shoes and clothes, is quite high. The trade areas of many central areas fail to reach this high level of threshold demand, so these services are absent. In general, shops selling goods which are bought very frequently, and services which are used very frequently, have a low threshold demand. It is obvious that confectionery is bought more often than furniture, so a confectioner's shop has a lower threshold demand than a furniture shop.

Central areas which possess only those services with a low threshold demand are said to be of low status; those which have services with a high threshold demand are said to be of high status.

Suggested Plan

In many towns, particularly those with a long history, the central area consists of a large number of very small properties in a maze of narrow streets. In these cases, the 1 : 2500 (25·344 inches to 1 mile) Ordnance Survey map is unsatisfactory. In all studies of central areas it is preferable to use the 1 : 1250 (50·688 inches to 1 mile) Ordnance Survey map. Each sheet of maps on this scale covers a considerable part of a central area and in some cases the whole of it. Unfortunately 1 : 1250 maps are not available for all towns. If one cannot be obtained the 1 : 2500 map should be enlarged.

Since changes tend to occur rapidly in central areas, it is almost certain that the published map will be out of date, so a certain amount of alteration will be necessary in the field.

As in the field mapping of a whole town, it is necessary to walk through the survey area and plot the function of every building. The survey may deal at first with the ground floors only, but later it may be extended to include first floors and others. A separate land use map should be drawn for each floor. Mapping in the central area is much slower than in the outer districts of a town. It is very rarely possible to block off groups of premises with the same function; often every building in a street has a different function. Information about the function of a building may have to be gained from signs painted on windows or from name plates on or inside doorways. Because of the difficulty of field mapping it is important not to attempt to map more than one floor in any single survey. Usually there is a great advantage in working in pairs; one person reads the map and makes the entries on it, and the other classifies the type of land use and reads off the shorthand symbol from the scheme instructions.

a) Survey Instructions

The central area should be surveyed under the following headings:

i) Shops

Each shop is allocated the general symbol S

together with an index number or letter to indicate the detailed type. A definition of a shop for the purposes of urban field work is given on page 21. A full list of shop types is given on page 46. The divisions in this list represent a convenient subdivision of shops into broad categories. For example, **SS** to **S8** are food shops, **S28** to **S36** are service shops, etc. This classification is sometimes useful in the studies which follow a field survey. Shops which are branches of a national multiple firm may be indicated by a ring round their appropriate symbols. Burton's, for example, may be plotted as (**S11**).

ii) Offices

All offices are given the general symbol **O** and this is accompanied by an index number to indicate the detailed type. A full list of office types is provided on pages 46-47. The divisions marked on the list indicate a subdivision of offices into broad types such as professional (**O1** to **O7**), financial (**O8** to **O12**), trade (**O13** to **O15**), transport (**O16** to **O18**), political (**O19** to **O21**), etc. As in the case of shops, this subdivision will be found to be useful in follow-up work. It should be noted that **O18** (other travel office) does not include a travel agency, which should be classified as a shop (**S29**).

iii) Entertainment

This is often an important feature of central area land use. The general symbol is **E**. Full instructions are given on page 21.

iv) Residence

Residence is relatively unimportant in central areas, but a considerable amount may be found on first floors above shops and offices. There is no point in trying to distinguish house types in the central area because there are so few. Premises used for residence should be allocated the general symbol **L** together with an explanatory word such as **flat**. Residential hotels should be labelled **H** unless the town is a holiday resort (see 'Resort Function' below).

v) Public Buildings

A great many of these are found in central areas. They should be mapped as indicated on page 21.

vi) Open Spaces

There are relatively few open spaces in the central area. Usually only about twenty per cent. of the total area is occupied by open spaces including streets, gardens, churchyards, car parks, etc. The name of the use of the open space should be labelled on the map.

vii) Industry

The scheme outlined on pages 20 and 21 should be used in the central area, and wherever possible the actual name of the industry should be recorded on the map.

viii) Resort Function

In a holiday resort, areas dominated by hotels and boarding houses should not be regarded as part of the central area. Usually one finds that they are quite distinct from the commercial part of the town. Occasionally, however, one may find isolated resort hotels in the midst of shops or offices, and upper floors of buildings may be used as holiday flats. All holiday residence facilities should be marked on the map by using the general symbol **R** together with an explanatory word such as **hotel** or **flats**.

ix) Derelict Land and Property

The instructions given on page 22 should be followed.

b) Summary of Survey Scheme for Use in the Field

i) Shops

Mark **S** in the field.
Colour Yellow on the final map.

Subdivide by adding a number or letter to the general field symbol **S**. This number or letter should also be printed over the yellow colour on the final map. *Ring* the symbol and number or letter if the shop is a branch of a national multiple chain.

SP   Petrol station
SS   Supermarket
S1   Self-service grocer
S2   Non-self-service grocer
S3   Butcher
S4   Fishmonger
S5   Greengrocer
S6   Confectioner (bread and cakes)
S7   Off-licence
S8   Other food shop (state type)
S9   Tobacconist, newsagent, sweets
S10   Boots and shoes
S11   Men's wear
S12   Women's wear and drapery
S13   Furniture, furnishings, carpets
S14   Radio, electrical goods, rentals
S15   Cycles, prams, accessories
S16   Hardware, china, glass, decorating materials
S17   Stationery, books
S18   Chemist, photographic goods
S19   Leather goods
S20   Sports goods
S21   Jewellery, watches, clocks
S22   Toys
S23   Fancy goods
S24   Other non-food shop (state type)
S25   Department store
S26   Variety store (e.g. Woolworth's)
S27   Other general store (state type)
S28   Caterer, restaurant, fish and chips, café, snack bar
S29   Travel agent
S30   Betting shop
S31   Hairdresser
S32   Boot and shoe repairs
S33   Laundry reception
S34   Launderette (washing machines)
S35   Dry cleaner
S36   Other service shop (state type)
S37   Gas and electricity showroom (state which)
S38   Car and motor cycle showroom
S39   Vacant shop

ii) Offices

Mark **O** in the field.
Colour Blue on the final map.

Subdivide by adding a number to the general field symbol **O**. This number should also be printed over the blue colour on the final map.

O1   Solicitor
O2   Estate agent
O3   Accountant
O4   Surveyor
O5   Engineer
O6   Architect
O7   Other professional office (state type)
O8   Insurance
O9   Bank
O10   Stocks and shares broker
O11   Building society
O12   Other financial office (state type)
O13   General merchant
O14   Trade in a particular commodity (state which)
O15   Other trade office (state type)
O16   Haulage contractor
O17   Bus and coach office
O18   Other travel office (state type)
O19   Society office (trade union, political party, etc.) (state type)
O20   Central government office (state type)

O21 Local government office (state type)
O22 Office services
O23 Other office (state type)
O24 Vacant office

iii) Entertainment

Mark **E** in the field.
Colour Orange on the final map.

Subdivide by adding a letter to the general field symbol **E**. This letter should also be printed over the orange colour on the final map.
EC Cinemas and theatres
ED Dance hall
EP Public house (not residential)
In all other cases label the *name* of the type of entertainment.

iv) Residence

Mark **L** in the field.
Colour Grey on the final map.

Do not subdivide residences.
Label **flats** by name.
H Residential hotel (not to be used in holiday resort).

v) Public Buildings

Mark the name in full both in the field and on the final map.
Colour Green on the final map.

No subdivision necessary.

vi) Open Spaces

Mark the name of their function in full both in the field and on the final map.

No subdivision necessary.

vii) Industry

Mark **I** in the field.
Colour Red on the final map.

Subdivide by adding a number to the general field symbol **I**. This number should also be printed over the red colour on the final map.
I1 Metal working, engineering, chemicals, glass, pottery, cement, etc.
I2 Textiles, leather goods, clothing.
I3 Food, drink, tobacco.
I4 Printing, manufacture of wood and paper.
I5 Service industry.
Any other industry – label **I**.
In all cases, label the *name* of the industry if possible.

viii) Resort Function

Mark **R** in the field.
Colour Purple on the final map.

Do not subdivide resort function.
Label **flats** and **hotel** by name.

ix) Derelict Land and Property

Mark the symbols given below both in the field and on the final map.
Do not colour the final map.

Outline the areas of each of the following categories and label with the symbols indicated.
DEM Building demolished. Insert the new use of the land if possible.

DER Building still standing but out of use and decaying.

5 Examples of the Field Study of the Central Area of a Town

The following three examples illustrate the varying size, form and status of the central areas of towns.

Longridge

a) Background Information

The small town of Longridge, Lancashire (population: about 5 700), situated about ten kilometres to the north–east of Preston, serves as a shopping and service centre for the farming area which lies between the river Ribble and the Bowland Fells. The town originally grew as a result of the importance of quarrying and the cotton industry during the nineteenth century, but now these industries have declined. Longridge appears to be developing as a dormitory town for Preston; most of the new houses are being built on the Preston side of the town. The town as a whole has about sixty to seventy shops, with an average annual turnover of about ten thousand pounds, and the greatest concentration of these is found in Berry Lane (fig. 11).

b) Summary of the Field Work Results

The results of the field mapping of the central area of Longridge are summarized in fig. 11. The various urban services are concentrated in a distance of about 270 m along Berry Lane, from the council offices in the south-east to the disused railway station in the north-west. The streets leading away from Berry Lane on each side are made up almost entirely of terraced residential property. This is a linear central area, extending along a single street, and it is interrupted in places by residential property. Even in the busiest part, next to the post office, there is a house used for residence only.

The Longridge Co-operative Society makes an important contribution to shopping facilities. Its large building on the south-west side of Berry Lane contains five shops selling women's wear, furniture, confectionery, men's wear and shoes; a smaller building contains a butcher's and a grocer's shop; and another shop, on the opposite side of Berry Lane, sells chemist's goods. This single group of shops therefore goes a long way towards providing for everyday needs and even makes provision for less frequent purchases such as furniture. Other shops include a self-service grocer, a greengrocer, two women's wear and drapery shops and three hairdressers (two for women and one for men). There is also a shop where home decorators can obtain wallpaper and paint (S16), and the electrical goods shop (S14)

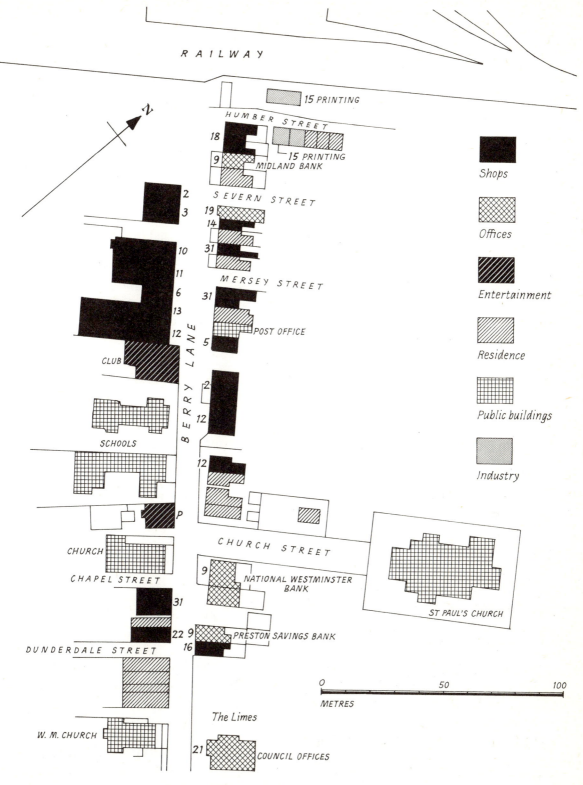

RAILWAY

15 PRINTING

HUMBER STREET

18
15 PRINTING
9 MIDLAND BANK

SEVERN STREET

2
3
19
14
10
31
11
6
MERSEY STREET
13
31
12
5 POST OFFICE
CLUB
2
12
SCHOOLS
12
P
CHURCH
CHURCH STREET
CHAPEL STREET
9 NATIONAL WESTMINSTER BANK
31
22 9 PRESTON SAVINGS BANK
DUNDERDALE STREET
16
BERRY LANE

St PAUL'S CHURCH

Shops

Offices

Entertainment

Residence

Public buildings

Industry

0   50   100
METRES

W. M. CHURCH
The Limes
21 COUNCIL OFFICES

Fig. 11   The Central Area of Longridge

also sells Calor gas supplies. The post office and another shop sell toys. Offices consist of three banks and the office of the co-operative society.

No pattern of distribution of offices or shop types can be recognized. The centre of activity appears to lie near the co-operative society building where most cars seem to park and the pavements are widest.

Longridge can therefore be classified as a service centre of fairly low status, catering mainly for the day to day needs of the population of the town and its surrounding area. It is, however, able to support a furniture and a men's wear shop, which may be regarded as having higher status.

Brixham

a) Background Information

Brixham (population: about 12 800) is situated opposite Torquay, on the south side of Tor Bay, and now forms part of the new county borough of Torbay in Devon. The town has long been an important fishing port, but since World War I the fishing industry has declined in importance. Fortunately the tourist industry has grown and the town is also a fairly important service centre for part of south-east Devon. Recent expansion of the town has been mostly eastwards, and consists of modern detached and semi-detached houses and flats, together with very large holiday camps. The central area is located on reclaimed land which forms a level strip extending inland from the harbour (fig. 12). Brixham as a whole has about one hundred and forty shops, with an average turnover of about thirteen thousand pounds.

b) Summary of the Field Work Results

The field survey takes in only the north-eastern part of Brixham's central area, extending inland from the harbour for about 270 m in a strip about 140 m wide. Brixham's central area here consists mainly of Fore Street and Middle Street (fig. 12). These two streets run along the foot of the very steep slopes of the valley; access to the upper slopes on each side is by means of steep hills such as St. Peter's Hill, or flights of steps, such as Cavern, Shinner's and Broad Steps (fig. 12). Relief features seem to have exerted a strong influence on the overall shape of the central area. Business activities are entirely confined to the level valley floor; the steep slopes are occupied by residential property. Brixham's central area is therefore clearly demarcated to the north-west and south-east.

The service area consists of a double line of shops and offices along Fore Street and a single line along Middle Street, these being linked by a transverse line along The Strand. In the centre is a bus station, an area of car parks and a fairly clearly recognizable industrial zone consisting mainly of warehouses and service industries. There is a marked contrast between the services provided in Middle Street and Fore Street. A notable feature of Middle Street is the very large number of shops selling fancy goods (S23), particularly at its north-east end, near The Strand. Offices are few, and the line of shops is sometimes interrupted by residential property (fig. 12). Fore Street, on the other hand, provides a much wider range of services. There are a large number of food shops (S1 to S8) and a concentration of cafés (S28) towards the harbour. Clothing shops (S10 to S12) are scattered along the length of the street and these include specialist men's wear shops (S11). The relatively high status of Brixham as a shopping centre is

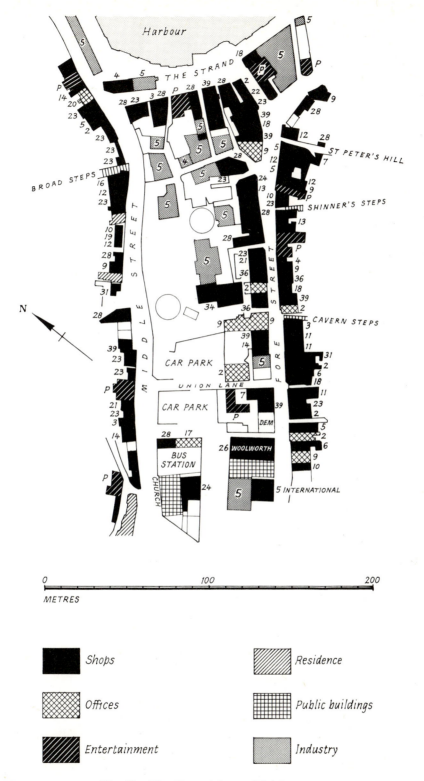

Fig. 12   The Central Area of Brixham

Shops

Offices

Entertainment

Residence

Public buildings

Industry

suggested by the presence of Woolworth's and the International Stores supermarket at the south-west end of Fore Street. Shops along The Strand consist mainly of food shops (**S2** and **S3**) and caterers (**S28**). These face the harbour.

Brixham has no separate office zone. Banks and estate agents are distributed along Fore Street, the main shopping street.

Bolton

a) Background Information

Bolton has a population of about 150 000. The town as a whole has about two thousand five hundred shops, with an average turnover of about twelve thousand pounds. It is a shopping and service centre for a densely populated area of well over 200 000. Over four hundred of Bolton's shops are situated in its central area and of these about a third are food shops and another third clothing shops. The central area food shops have an average turnover of about twenty-two thousand pounds and the clothing shops about thirty-three thousand pounds.

Only the north-eastern part of Bolton's central area has been included in the survey (fig. 13). The major street framework here consists of Knowsley Street – Oxford Street – Victoria Square, Bridge Street and Bradshawgate running roughly from north to south, and these are linked by the east-west trending Deansgate. The spaces between these major streets are occupied by a maze of narrow streets and alleys, particularly in the south of the survey area between Bradshawgate and Victoria Square (fig. 13). Here, much rebuilding has already taken place and there are plans for an important urban renewal scheme in the Fold Street area. Oxford Street and Victoria Square are soon to become part of Bolton's first pedestrian precinct.

b) Summary of the Field Work Results

The survey area is approximately 270 m square. In contrast to Brixham, central area service functions cover the entire area; there are no ground floor residences anywhere. A brief examination of fig. 13 indicates that there is a broad zoning of urban functions. Shops and offices occupy practically the whole of the major street frontages, only interrupted occasionally by public houses (**P**). An office zone can be clearly seen in the Fold Street area. Former industrial property in the north-east is now derelict, and the main industrial premises are those to the east of Mealhouse Lane which are concerned with the production and distribution of Bolton's daily and weekly newspapers (fig. 13).

Food shops (**SS** and **S1** to **S8**) (fig. 14a) have a scattered distribution and nearly all are housed in small premises, the co-operative society supermarket in Bridge Street being the main exception. Grocers (**S1** and **S2**), butchers (**S3**), a fishmonger (**S4**) a greengrocer (**S5**) and confectioners (**S6**) are all present. Most of these would be found in central areas of smaller towns than Bolton. Bolton's relatively high status is suggested by the existence of specialist food shops such as the Health Food shop (**S2**) in Hotel Street and four specialist wine shops (**S7**) (fig. 14a).

In contrast to the food shops, the clothing and footwear shops (fig. 14b) tend to occupy the frontages of the major shopping streets and some can be seen to occupy large premises. They also show a marked tendency to occupy corner sites at junctions of important streets. The busiest point in Bolton's central area is the junction of

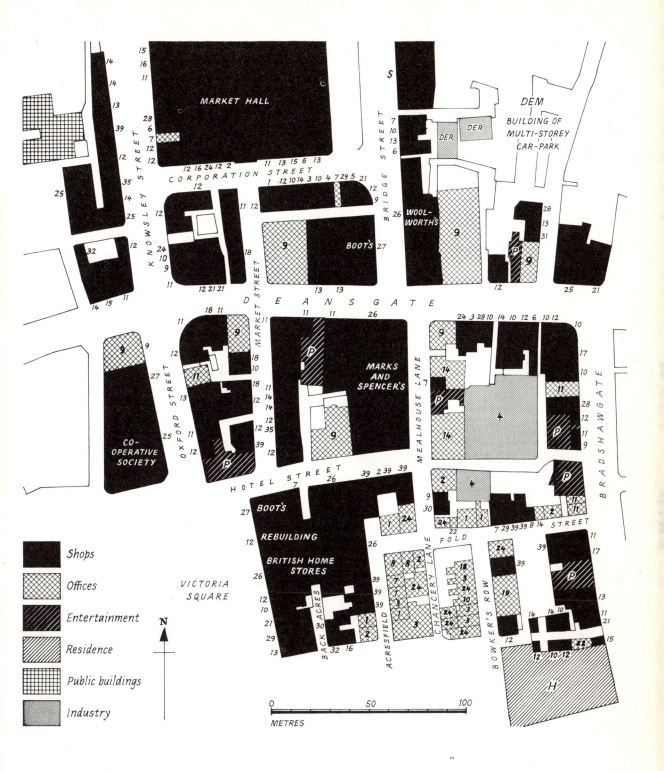

Fig. 13   The Central Area of Bolton

Deansgate with Knowsley Street and Oxford Street. Three of the corner sites at this junction are occupied by multiple men's wear shops (Alexandre, John Collier and Jackson); the busy Deansgate – Market Street corner site is occupied by Burton. The large number of specialist men's wear shops is an indication of Bolton's high status as a service centre.

Household shops in the survey area are relatively few (fig. 14c), but large furniture shops (S13) tend to occupy favoured sites, such as the premises of New Day and Wade in Deansgate, and Woodhouse in Victoria Square.

The majority of Bolton's large general stores are situated in the survey area (fig. 14d), all occupying very prominent sites. Woolworth's, Boot's and the very large new Marks and Spencer's building dominate the busy Deansgate – Bridge Street junction; Boot's, British Home Stores and the Co-operative Society department store are prominently placed in Victoria Square. It should be noted that the new British Home Stores has been built over Back Acres, formerly a narrow lane (fig. 13). Old street patterns are sometimes inadequate for a modern central area.

There is a distinct office zone in Bolton's central area, and the major categories of offices have contrasting distributions.

This can only occur in a central area of fairly high status with a considerable number of offices. Fig. 14e shows that financial offices (O8 to O12) are generally separate from professional offices (O1 to O7). Banks (O9) and building societies (O11) usually occupy sites on the main shopping streets. Banks particularly have gained important street junction sites, such as those occupied by the National Westminster at the Deansgate – Oxford Street junction, Barclay's and Williams Deacon's at the Deansgate– Market Street junction, and the Midland where Mealhouse Lane meets Deansgate. Professional offices tend to be concentrated in the narrow Fold Street, Acresfield, Chancery Lane and Bowker's Row (fig. 14e). These are mostly solicitors (O1) and accountants (O3), but there is also a private enquiry agent (O7). Two financial offices are found in this professional office zone; these are an insurance office (O8) and a stocks and shares broker (O10). The professional offices in Knowsley Street and Corporation Street (O7) are the premises of specialist opticians.

An interesting pattern is formed by mapping the distribution of vacant shops and vacant offices (fig. 14f). In this area, premises are vacant either because they are in new buildings which have not yet been let or because they are in very old buildings which are likely to be demolished in the near future.

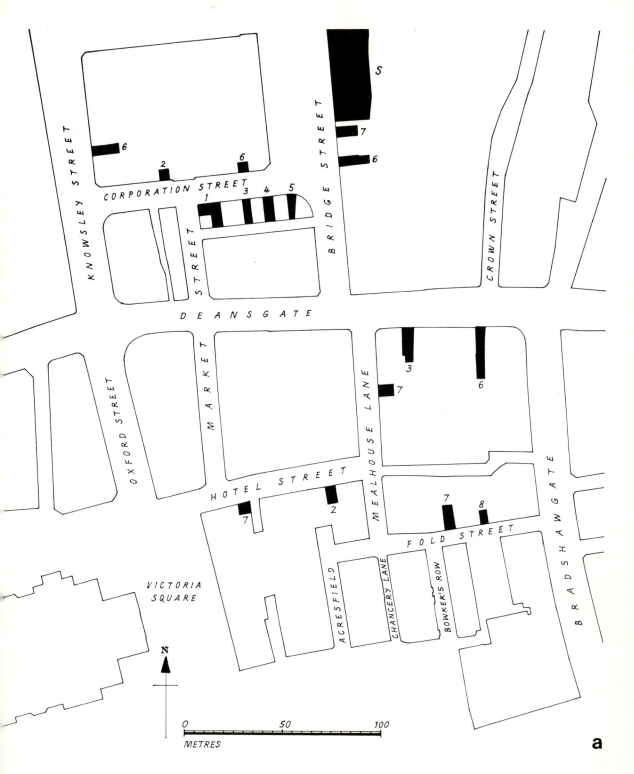

Fig. 14a   The Distribution of Food Shops in the Central Area of Bolton

a

Fig. 14b   The Distribution of Boot and Shoe and Clothing Shops in the Central Area of Bolton

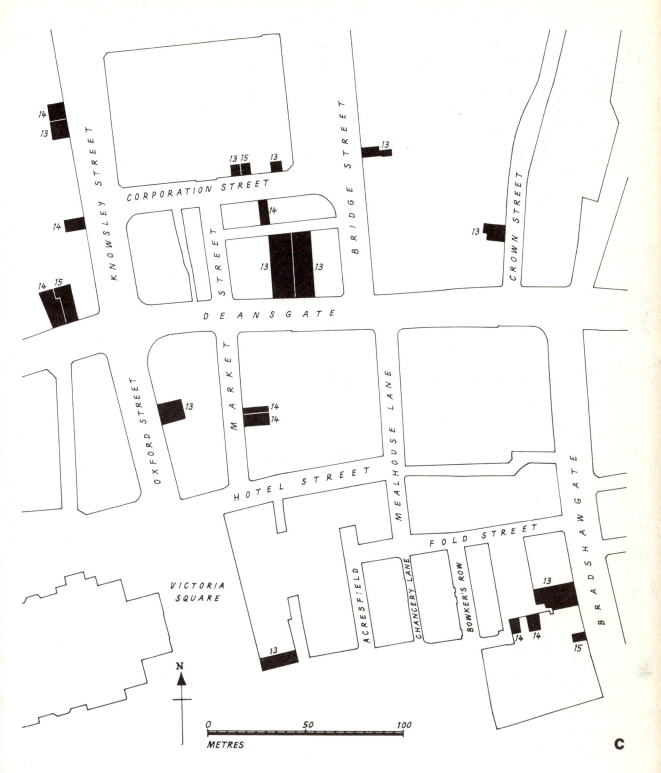

Fig. 14c   The Distribution of Household Goods Shops in the Central Area of Bolton

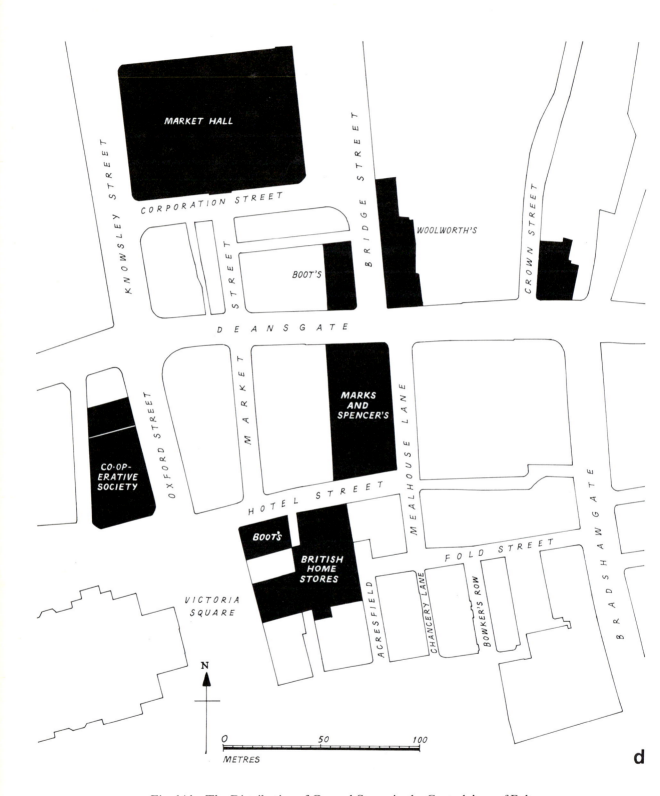

Fig. 14d   The Distribution of General Stores in the Central Area of Bolton

d

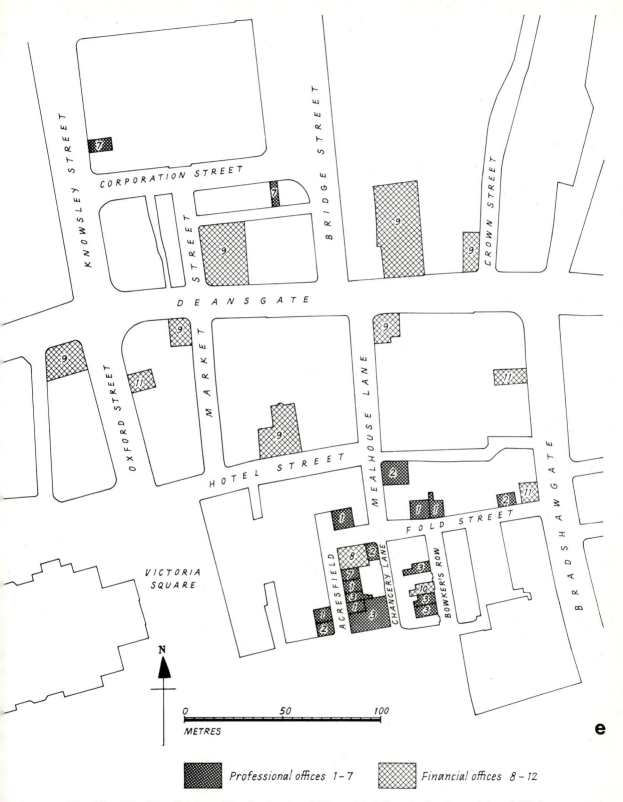

Fig. 14e   The Distribution of Professional and Financial Offices in the Central Area of Bolton

e

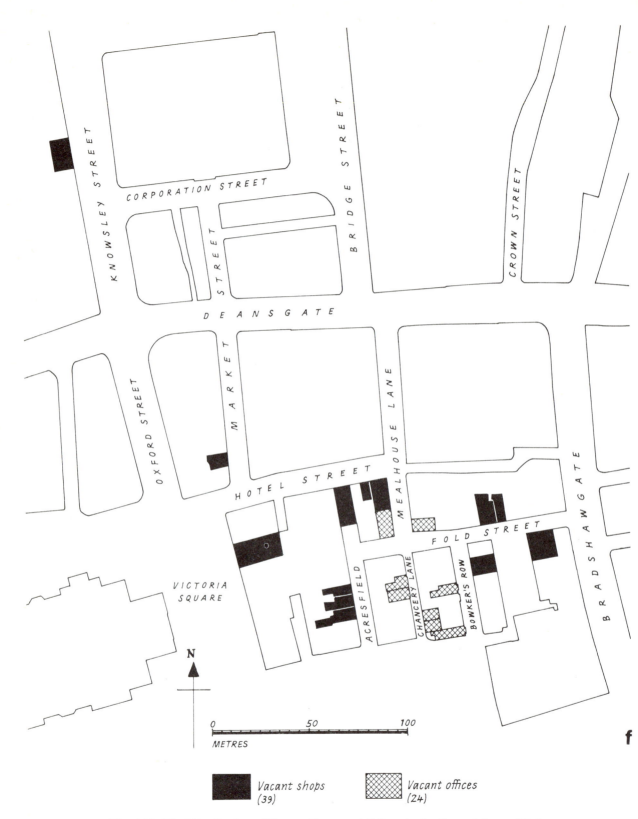

Fig. 14f The Distribution of Vacant Shops and Offices in the Central Area of Bolton

Exercises

1   Make an assessment of the efficiency of the central area of your town from the point of view of (a) the pedestrian shopper, and (b) the visiting motorist.
The following points should be considered:
a) *the pedestrian shopper*
    (i) the location of the bus station and the railway station in relation to the main shopping area,
    (ii) the location of markets in relation to shops,
    (iii) the difficulties of pedestrian movement, the presence of barriers such as streets crowded with vehicles,
    (iv) the grouping of large shops such as department and variety stores, and of shops and restaurants.
b) *the visiting motorist*
    (i) size and accessibility of car parks,
    (ii) the location of car parks in relation to the main shopping area,
    (iii) the pattern of one-way streets,
    (iv) restrictions on street parking in the central area.

2   Count the number of pedestrians who pass various points in the central area of your town in periods of ten minutes on a busy day. Relate the differences in pedestrian flow with the types of shops which are found near the points where you make the counts.

3   Using figs. 11 and 12 and the material in chapter 5, make a list of contrasts between the central areas of Longridge and Brixham. Suggest reasons why these contrasts exist.

4   Explain the evidence provided in fig. 12 that Fore Street is a shopping street of higher status than Middle Street in the central area of Brixham.

5   How do you think that the tourist industry has influenced the characteristics of the central area of Brixham?

6   Refer to figs. 12 and 13. What signs are there on these maps that Bolton's central area has a higher status than that of Brixham?

7   Using fig. 13, trace the major street pattern of Bolton's central area. Summarize fig. 13 by dividing the area into (a) shopping and banking zone, (b) office zone, (c) industrial zone.

8   Compare figs. 14a, 14b and 14c. Suggest reasons why food shops are rarely found on the main street frontages but clothing and furniture shops commonly are.

6 The Field Study of Suburban Service Centres

General Principles

Suburban service centres are places distributed throughout a town where buyers and sellers exchange goods and services. They are quite distinct from a town's central area. Usually a suburban service centre consists of a group of shops, possibly including a co-operative society store and a branch post office, associated with public houses, offices of certain types and possibly a branch lending library or a social club.

Suburban service centres are central places (page 39) of lower status than the central area itself. Buyers from a fairly small trade area within the town come here to make regular day to day purchases of goods and services. These are goods and services which are not worth making a longer journey to obtain. Each purchase is likely to cost little, but purchases are very frequent.

a) The Form of Suburban Service Centres

Suburban service centres vary greatly in size and composition. The number, size and variety of shops and other service establishments depend upon the spending power of the people who live in their trade areas. Various broad types of suburban service centres may be recognized:

1. Major roads leading outwards from the centre of a town are often flanked by lines of shops, especially in the older, inner part of the town. These can be regarded as suburban service centres in a linear form. At first sight separate centres may be difficult to define, but a closer study will reveal that it is possible to recognize gaps, occupied by residences, mills, waste land and parks, between separate areas of service establishments.

2. Nucleated groups of shops may be found within an area of older housing. A small group may consist of a grocer and an off-licence on adjacent street corners; larger centres may have shops extending outwards for a short distance from a street intersection.

3. New council housing estates often have a planned group of shops placed centrally within the estate, and privately owned estates often contain groups of shops.

4. Areas of twentieth century expansion in a town may have completely surrounded a pre-existing village. In this case, the centre of the old village may have become a suburban service centre. Shops and other service establishments, originally designed to serve the needs of the village, expand to meet the increased demand.

5. Planned service centres of a considerable size may be developed near the outskirts of a town. These will have large car parks and

shops and offices set in an area restricted to pedestrian traffic.

b) The Composition of Suburban Service Centres

Suburban service centres are composed mostly of shops. Few offices, apart from banks and minor trade offices, are found outside the central area.

There are more shops in suburban service areas than in the central area. In most towns eighty per cent. or so of their shops are found outside their central areas. The great majority of a town's food shops are found outside the central area. Hence suburban service centres often contain grocers, butchers, greengrocers, confectioners and off-licences and these are found together with newsagents, household hardware shops and hairdressers, all of which have little reason to seek a central area location. All the above shop types are examples of those at which purchases are made very frequently, and their threshold demand (page 43) is quite low. Certain other types of shops are more characteristic of central areas than suburban service centres. Shops selling men's clothing, shoes and furniture tend to congregate in central areas where they usually occupy prominent sites. Jewellers, booksellers and chemists are also relatively few in suburban service centres. These 'central area' types of shops have a fairly high threshold demand and therefore tend only to be found in the larger suburban service centres which serve trade areas of high spending power.

Shops in suburban service areas are generally smaller and have a smaller turnover than those in central areas. Clearly, a smaller shop tends to have a lower threshold demand than a larger one and hence is more likely to exist in a suburban area where demand is relatively low. This is particularly the case in shops selling men's and women's clothing, and shoes and jewellery, in which there is a great contrast in size and turnover between the small suburban shop, often owner-managed, and the large central area establishment, often a branch of a nation-wide multiple firm. In the case of food shops there is not the same contrast. Suburban greengrocer shops are frequently as large as those in the central area.

The characteristics of suburban service areas also tend to vary according to social conditions within their trade areas. In a modern, privately owned housing estate one may find a number of banks, a specialist wine shop and possibly the office of a driving school. In older, inner parts of the town, household hardware shops, public houses and betting shops may be more common.

Suggested Plan

The basis of the field study is the counting of the number of service establishments which exist in each suburban service centre. There is little point in mapping functions building by building, since suburban service centres are so small that no recognizable internal patterns will appear. The purpose of the field study is to discover the overall pattern created by different service centres as they are scattered through the town and to relate this pattern to the general urban environment.

a) Survey Instructions

A copy of the 1 : 10560 (6 inches to 1 mile) Ordnance Survey map is useful to fix the location of the service centres.

The main problem in surveying in the field is to distinguish the different service areas, particularly where they have a linear form along a main road. There is no simple rule which can be applied here; the surveyor must make his own judgement on where one service area ends and another begins. He must look for every clue which suggests that a particular group of shops 'belong' together. Shops within any single service area may be separated from each other by a few residences, but the impression must be that movement between them is easy and convenient. In making this judgement, the surveyor should study the pattern of pedestrian movement and of the parking of cars, etc.

Once a particular service area has been identified, a count is made of the numbers of the various types of service establishments found within it. It is usually best to define a service area as possessing at least four shops in close proximity.

A sheet of paper is prepared with the list of establishments given opposite arranged in a column down the left-hand side. Other columns on the page are allocated to different service areas. A count is then made by inspecting each service establishment and placing a stroke on the line allocated to its type. At the end of the field survey the numbers of strokes on each line are totalled, thus giving the total number of each type of service establishment in the particular service centre. An example is given in Table 1.

The survey scheme for suburban service centres uses fundamentally the same classification of shops as was used in central area studies. It also involves the same broad categories of banks, other offices, public houses and other services (such as social clubs, libraries, etc). In the case of suburban centres, however, a separate category of co-operative society grocer is included because this type of shop is particularly

common in suburban service centres. Special care should be taken with certain categories of shops:

S5 A greengrocer who also sells fish should be classified as a greengrocer.

S7 A shop selling alcoholic drink should be thus classified even though it may also sell groceries.

S9 This includes branch post offices which usually also sell stationery and sweets. It should also include shops selling a wide variety of goods, including sweets, tobacco, stationery and toys.

S16 Shops selling crockery, pans, garden supplies, timber, 'do-it-yourself' supplies, plumber's goods, paint and wallpaper are all in this category.

S24 These include specialist pet shops, florists, etc.

Petrol stations should be ignored because it is unlikely that they will serve local trade areas only.

b) Summary of Survey Scheme for Use in the Field

The following list should be written down the left-hand side of the logging sheet:

SS Supermarket
S1 Self-service grocer
S2 Non-self-service grocer
S3 Butcher
S4 Fishmonger
S5 Greengrocer
S6 Confectioner (bread and cakes)
S7 Off-licence
Co-op Grocer
S8 Other food shop (note type)
S9 Tobacconist, newsagent, sweets, post office
S10 Boots and shoes
S11 Men's wear
S12 Women's wear and drapery

S13 Furniture, furnishings, carpets
S14 Radio, electrical goods, rentals
S15 Cycles, prams, accessories
S16 Hardware, china, glass, decorating and gardening materials, 'do it yourself' goods
S17 Stationery, books
S18 Chemist, photographic goods
S19 Leather goods
S20 Sports goods
S21 Jewellery, watches, clocks
S22 Toys
S23 Fancy goods
S24 Other non-food shop (note type)
S25 Department store
S26 Variety store (e.g. Woolworth's)
S27 Other general store (note type)
S28 Caterer, restaurant, fish and chips, café, snack bar

S29 Travel agent
S30 Betting shop
S31 Hairdresser
S32 Boot and shoe repairs
S33 Laundry (clothing left here)
S34 Launderette (washing machines)
S35 Dry cleaner
S36 Other service shop (note type)
S37 Gas and electricity showroom (note which)
S38 Car and motor cycle showroom
S39 Vacant shop

Banks
Other offices (note type)
Public houses
Other services (note type)

Table 1 The Field Study of Suburban Service Centres – Example of a Logging Sheet

Type of Service	Location of Service Centre			
	Crompton Way–Tonge Moor Rd.			
Food Shops				
SS Supermarket				
S1 SS Grocer				
S2 NSS Grocer	/			
S3 Butcher	/			
S4 Fishmonger				
S5 Greengrocer	/			
S6 Confectioner	/			
S7 Off-licence	/			
Co-op Grocer	/			
S8 Other Food Shop				
S9 Tobacconist, Newsagent, Sweets, P.O.	//			
Clothing Shops				
S10 Shoes				
S11 Men's Wear				
S12 Women's Wear & Drapery	/			
Household Shops				
S13 Furniture, Carpets, etc.				

Type of Service	Location of Service Centre			
	Crompton Way–Tonge Moor Rd.			
S14 Radio, Electrical	/			
S15 Cycles, Prams etc.				
S16 Hardware, China, Glass, Paint, etc.	/			
S17 Stationery, Books etc.				
S18 Chemist	/			
S19 Leather Goods				
S20 Sports Goods				
S21 Jewellery, Watches etc.				
S22 Toys				
S23 Fancy Goods				
S24 Other household				
Large Stores				
S25 Department Store				
S26 Variety Store				
S27 Other				
Service Shops				
S28 Café etc.	/ /			
S29 Travel Agent				
S30 Betting Shop				
S31 Hairdresser (State M or W)	/ W			
S32 Shoe Repair				
S33 Laundry				
S34 Launderette				
S35 Dry Cleaner				
S36 Other Service				
S37 Gas/Electricity Showroom				
S38 Car/Cycle Showroom				
S39 Vacant Shop				
Banks				
Other Offices				
Public Houses	/			
Other Service				

7 An Example of the Field Study of Suburban Service Centres

North Bolton

The survey area comprises the northern part of Bolton and a number of villages to the north. The growth of a considerable part of this area has already been outlined (page 14, fig. 3) and the broad pattern of its urban functions has been described (pages 17 and 18, fig. 6).

a) Background Information

Settlement in this area is more or less confined to the interfluves flanking the almost unpopulated valleys of the Eagley and Bradshaw Brooks. Two major north-south roads, Blackburn Road and Tonge Moor-Turton-Darwen Road, follow the interfluves and eventually converge in the north near Egerton (fig. 15). The main east-west link between these roads is Crompton Way, which crosses the industrial southern part of the valley of the Eagley Brook. These three roads carry a great deal of traffic.

Densely populated areas of terraced housing extend northwards on each side of Blackburn Road as far as Astley Bridge, and in a narrow strip along Tonge Moor Road to beyond its junction with Crompton Way. Flanking these older residential areas, and beyond them to the north, are modern housing estates (fig. 15). In the far north a number of old village centres, Egerton,

Bromley Cross, Bradshaw, and Harwood, are aligned roughly from north-west to south-east along the line of Darwen-Turton Road (fig. 15). Many large new housing estates have been built around these villages, and development is continuing rapidly.

b) The Field Survey

i) The Service Centres

For the purposes of this survey a suburban service centre has been defined as a group of service establishments containing at least four shops. Twenty three such service centres have been identified in the area. The locations of these are indicated in fig. 15.

Shops and other service establishments are distributed fairly continuously along Blackburn Road south of Astley Bridge, and rather more intermittently along Tonge Moor Road south of Crompton Way. Slight gaps of fifty to one hundred metres in the continuity of the shops have permitted centres W, R, T, U, C and A to be identified along Blackburn Road. Both of centres T and U, for example, are situated in the urban area of Astley Bridge. It has been possible to distinguish them as separate centres because of the existence of school buildings and demolished property between them (figs. 15 and 7b). Thus, the centres between W and A along Blackburn Road, and between

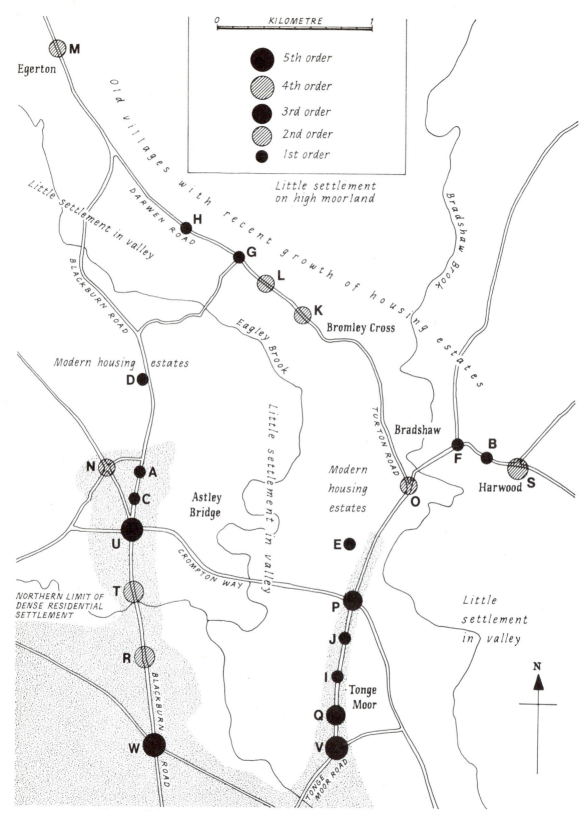

Fig. 15   The Distribution of the Suburban Service Centres of North Bolton

V and P along Tonge Moor Road, are examples of the linear type of suburban service centre.

Towards the northern part of the survey area other types of centres are found. Centre E is a small group of shops in a modern council housing estate, and centre D is a similar group in a modern privately owned estate. Centres M, H, G, L, O, F and B consist mostly of shops occupying older property in old village centres (fig. 15). Centre K at Bromley Cross comprises a small group of modern shops in close proximity to large new housing estates. Centre S at Harwood is a large modern shopping and service centre with a very large car park and a traffic-free pedestrian area giving access to all the shops.

ii) The Survey

A count has been made of the numbers of the various types of shops and other service establishments found in each service centre. Totals for each centre have been set out in the form of a table (Table 2, page 71) the smallest centres being on the left and the largest on the right.

iii) Summary of the Field Work Results

A Classification of the Suburban Service Centres. Service centres in the survey area vary in size from two which have only four shops to a very large centre with seventy shops, a greater number than some towns. If centres A, C, T and U, which are all close to one another in Astley Bridge, are grouped together as one centre it has ninety four shops. There appears to be only one sharp break in the series of shop totals which could be used as a means of classifying the service centres. This occurs between centres T and U which have a difference in total shops of twenty one (Table 2). When a count is

made of the numbers of different *types* of shops in each centre, the basis of a classification which combines both total numbers of shops and variety of shops immediately appears. The twenty three centres have therefore been classified into the following orders of importance:

Order	Total Number of Shops	Number of Different Shop Types
5	53 and over	23
4	25–32	17–18
3	15–20	12–13
2	9–12	8–9
1	4–6	3–6

If centres A, C, T and U were regarded as a single service centre in Astley Bridge, this would have a much higher status than the above, since it would have ninety four shops in twenty seven different types.

This classification of suburban service centres is more obvious if a scatter graph is made of the relationship between 'Total Shops' and 'Total Different Shop Types' (fig. 16). On this graph the five orders of service centres in north Bolton are clearly separated by distinct 'breaks'.

Characteristics of the Suburban Service Centres. A study of Table 2 brings out the major characteristics of these suburban service centres. The most common services provided are S16 (Hardware, etc.), S9 (Newsagent, etc.), S31 (Hairdresser), S2 (Grocer), S3 (Butcher) and S5 (Greengrocer). All these are carried on in more than twenty five establishments within the twenty three service areas. There are no examples of S25–S27 (large general stores), S19 (Leather goods) or S29 (Travel agent). Also, S20 (Sports goods), S23 (Fancy goods) and S4 (Fishmonger) are very rare, though many of the greengrocers sell fish as a sideline.

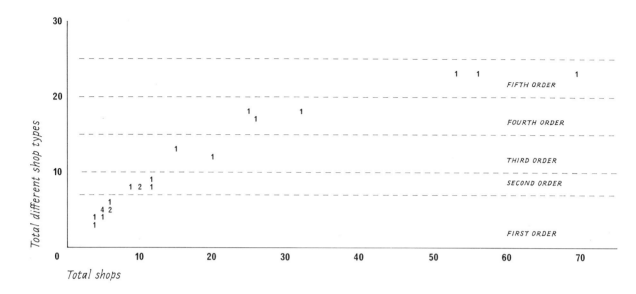

Fig. 16   A Scatter Graph Showing the Classification of the Suburban Service Centres of North Bolton

Different types of shops tend to occur in service centres of different status. Certain types of shops tend to occur frequently in small service centres. Examples of these are most of the food shops (S1 to S8), S9 (Newsagent, etc.), S12 (Women's wear), S28 (particularly fish and chip shops), and S31 (particularly ladies' hairdressers). Fairly typical of a small service centre is centre E which has a grocer, a greengrocer, a confectioner, a newsagent and a fish and chip shop. In larger service centres where demand may be much greater, it is possible for shops with a higher threshold demand to be established. Thus, in larger centres, S18 (Chemist), S34 (Launderette) and S14 (Radio, etc.) begin to appear. In the largest centres of all, shops such as SS (Supermarket), S11 (Men's wear), S15 (Cycles, etc.), S10 (Shoes), and

S21 (Jewellers) appear. These are types of shops which are characteristic of the central areas of towns, and tend to be found only in large suburban shopping centres. The largest centres of the survey area also contain a variety of specialist shops. Centre W is the only one to contain a specialist fishmonger (S4). The 'other non-food shops' (S24) found in the large centres are florists. Other service shops (S36) found in the large centres are two specialist photographers, a television set repair depot and a dog beautician.

In general, in the small suburban service centres, food shops (S1 to S8) and newsagents form a high proportion of the total number of shops. In the larger centres the occurrence of clothing (S10 to S12), household (S13 to S16) and non-food shops (S17 to S24) tends to increase.

Other urban services apart from shops become important in the larger fourth and fifth order centres (Table 2). Other offices are usually the surgeries of doctors and dentists, though the planned suburban service centre (S) has an estate agent and the office of a driving school.

The Pattern of Suburban Service Centres. The status of suburban service centres in general diminishes northwards towards the edge of the built-up area (fig. 15). This is well illustrated by the sequence from V (fifth order) to Q (third order) to I and J (first order) northwards along Tonge Moor Road. The population density of the trade areas of the various centres also tends to decrease northwards, so that service centres are smaller and more widely spaced. The exception is the second order centre (S) at Harwood which appears to have arisen in response to the increased demand resulting from the extensive building of housing estates in the area.

Table 2 Suburban Service Centres of North Bolton – Composition

		A	B	C	D	E	F	G	H	I	J	K	L	M	N	O	P	Q	R	S	T	U	V	W
SS	Supermarket		1																	1		1	1	
S1	SS Grocer																							
S2	Grocer					1	1			2	1		2	1	1	2	1	4	2	1	2	2	3	1
S3	Butcher			1	1				1			1	1	1	2	1	1	1	2		1	5	4	4
S4	Fishmonger																							1
S5	Greengrocer			1	1	1		1	1					1	2	1	1	2	1	1	3	1	3	2
S6	Confectioner				1	1						1			1	1	1	1	1	1	2	3	3	2
S7	Off-licence								1				1	1		1	1	1	1			2		
	Co-op Grocer			1					1			1		1	1		1							
S8	Other Food																					1		
Total Food		0	1	2	4	3	1	2	3	2	1	3	4	5	7	5	6	9	7	5	8	12	17	10
S9	Tobacco etc.	1	1	1	1	1	0	1	1	1	2	1	1	2	1	2	2	1	2	2	3	6	5	6
S10	Shoes																	1	1			1	1	1
S11	Men's Wear																	1	1	1	1			
S12	Women's Wear	1	1						1		1	1	1	2		1	1	2		1		7	8	6
Total Clothing		1	1	0	0	0	0	0	1	0	1	1	1	2	0	1	1	3	1	1	2	9	10	7
S13	Furniture																			1	2		2	2
S14	Radio etc.															1		1	1	2	1	1		4
S15	Cycles etc.																	1	1				1	1
S16	Hardware						1		1	1	1	2	1	1	2	2	1	2	3	3	3	4	5	13
S17	Books																		1	1				1
S18	Chemist											1				1	1	1	1			2	1	1
S19	Leather																							
S20	Sports																				1			
S21	Jewellery etc.																	1	1		1			
S22	Toys																							
S23	Fancy Goods																				1			
S24	Other Non-food																					2	1	2
Total Household		0	0	0	0	0	1	0	1	1	1	3	1	1	2	2	3	4	7	7	9	12	11	24

	A	B	C	D	E	F	G	H	I	J	K	L	M	N	O	P	Q	R	S	T	U	V	W
S25 Department Store																							
S26 Variety Store																							
S27 Other general																							
Total General	0	0	0	0	0	0	0	0	0	0	0	0	0	0	0	0	0	0	0	0	0	0	0
S28 Café etc.		1			1	1	1		1					1		2		1	2	1	1	3	3
S29 Travel Agent																							
S30 Betting			1															1			1	2	2
S31 Hairdresser	2		1		2		1	1		2				1	2	1	3	2	1	2	5	4	6
S32 Shoe Repair											1								1				
S33 Laundry																							
S34 Launderette						1												2	1	1	1	1	1
S35 Dry Cleaner									1									1			1	1	1
S36 Other Service																		2					2
Total Service	2	1	2	0	1	3	2	0	2	1	1	3	0	2	2	3	3	6	5	6	10	11	15
S37 Gas/Electricity																							
S38 Car/Cycle																		1		1			2
Total Showrooms	0	0	0	0	0	0	0	0	0	0	0	0	0	0	0	0	0	1	0	1	0	0	2
S39 Vacant																		1	6	3	4	2	6
Total Shops	4	4	5	5	5	5	5	6	6	6	9	10	10	12	12	15	20	25	26	32	53	56	70
Total different shop types	3	4	5	5	5	4	5	6	6	5	5	8	8	8	9	8	13	12	18	17	18	23	23
Banks						1								1					2	1	2	2	1
Other Offices								1									1	3	2	2	2		3
Public Houses			1									1		1	1			1	1	3	3	1	6
Other Services			1		1	1										1				1	3	1	

Exercises

1 Which of the suburban service centres located in fig. 15 would you expect (a) to increase, (b) to decrease in importance in the future? Suggest reasons.

2 Suggest reasons why the service centres along Tonge Moor Road seem to be generally of lower status than those along Blackburn Road (fig. 15).

3 Describe briefly the locations of the highest order service centres as shown in fig. 15. What do they have in common?

4 Using Table 2, construct scatter graphs like Fig. 16 showing the following relationships:
   a) 'total food shops' and 'total shops',
   b) 'total clothing shops' and 'total shops',
   c) 'total household shops' and 'total shops',
   d) 'total service shops' and 'total shops',
   What conclusions seem to emerge?

5 List four types of shops in Table 2 which appear to have a very high threshold demand, and four others which appear to have a very low threshold demand. Explain your choice.

8 The Field Study of the Sphere of Influence of a Town

General Principles

The aim of this type of field study is to investigate the social and economic influence of the town on its surrounding area. The area surrounding a town of considerable size will consist partly of open countryside, perhaps with some villages and hamlets, and partly of smaller towns. For this area the town provides facilities for entertainment, employment, shopping, business etc. This area, which is to a great extent dependent upon the town, is known as the town's sphere of influence. Other terms which mean more or less the same thing are 'urban field', 'service area' and 'trade area'. The purpose of a field study is to investigate the extent and the nature of this area.

In chapters six and seven we have studied the suburban service areas of a town. Each of these has a sphere of influence, of course, but its extent is usually quite small and is usually entirely within the built-up area of the town. In studying the sphere of influence of a *town* we are thinking primarily about its central area rather than its suburban service centres. Here are found the services of high status for which people make considerable journeys from the surrounding area. It is unlikely, for example, that very many people outside the town will make a deliberate journey to visit a snack bar or a ladies' hairdresser in a small suburban service centre, unless of course the establishment concerned is known to provide a specialist service of particular excellence. On the other hand, the large department stores, furniture shops, jewellers and gas and electricity showrooms of the town's central area, may attract customers from a wide area. These types of shops are rarely found in suburban service centres (page 63, Table 2). It is possible that some important urban services are located outside the actual central area of the town and that these are of great importance to the surrounding area. Large football grounds, for example, are not usually located in central areas, yet their influence may extend for many kilometres. Supporters of Nottingham Forest, for example, travel over one hundred kilometres to matches from the Lincolnshire coast at Skegness. Similarly a large industrial enterprise, possibly on the outskirts of the town, may employ people from a wide area; also a large bakery outside the central area may make deliveries to far distant towns and villages. Hence, in considering the sphere of influence of a town, we must not confine our attention solely to influences originating in the central area, important though these may be.

There are many problems involved in the study of a town's sphere of influence. For instance, it is impossible to draw a line on a map which exactly marks its extent.

a) A large town provides many different services of different status (pages 43 and 44). A department store, for example, provides a service of high status and customers may travel great distances to visit it. A central area greengrocer, on the other hand, provides only a low status service and his service area may be restricted to quite a small part of the town. He will compete with other greengrocers in suburban service areas, whereas a department store will usually have little competition from other areas because department stores are not usually found in either suburban service areas or small towns and villages outside the major town. Thus, it is likely that each service provided by the town will have its own particular service area, and the higher the status of this service the larger its service area.

The sphere of influence of a town, therefore, tends to consist of a large number of service areas of individual services arranged in roughly concentric rings around the town (fig. 17a). The town itself and the area immediately adjoining it are dominated by the town's influence. This influence decreases as the perimeter of each successive service area is crossed. Finally, on the outer edge of the town's sphere of influence, links with the town may only exist in terms of services of very high status.

b) The shape of a town's sphere of influence may be influenced by various factors. An important influence is the presence of other towns which provide similar services. If there are two towns located close enough together for their service areas in respect of particular services to overlap (fig. 17b), an area will exist where the two towns compete with one another. Hence, it is likely that each town will restrict the full development of the other's sphere of influence since they will both have to share the zone of competition which lies between them. On the other hand,

if there are no competing towns for a considerable distance, a town's sphere of influence may extend far across the countryside until it is eventually limited by sheer distance.

A study of Bolton's sphere of influence reveals that it extends much further northward and north-westward than south-eastward. The presence of Manchester, eighteen kilometres away to the south-east, restricts the development of Bolton's sphere of influence in this direction.

c) Other influences on the shape of a town's sphere of influence are transport facilities. Good roads and bus and railway services may extend a town's influence in certain directions because they make it easier for people to travel to the town.

d) The sphere of influence of a large town may enclose the various smaller spheres of influence of smaller towns. It is possible, for example, for a large town to provide a high status service which smaller towns cannot provide. Hence the sphere of influence of the large town in respect of the high status service may enclose the spheres of influence of smaller towns in respect of services of lower status (fig. 17c). For example, the sphere of influence of a First Division football club may contain many smaller spheres of influence of clubs which belong to minor leagues.

Suggested Plan

The nature and extent of the sphere of influence of a town may be investigated in two different ways. One of these is by carrying out field work *within the town*. This involves either visiting certain enterprises in the town which are known to provide services for the surrounding area, or

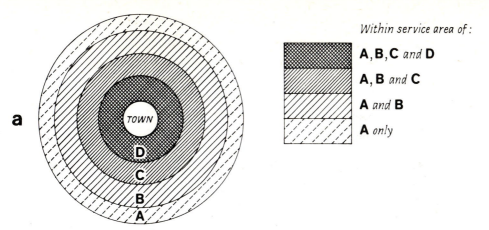

Within service area of :

■ A, B, C and D
▬ A, B and C
▨ A and B
▨ A only

Fig. 17a   The Varying Extent of the Sphere of Influence in Relation to the Status of the Service Provided.

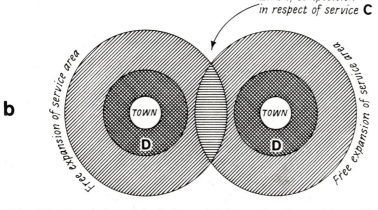

Zone of competition in respect of service **C**

Free expansion of service area

Free expansion of service area

Fig. 17b   The Restriction of the Sphere of Influence by Competition with a Neighbouring Town

STATUS OF SERVICES

Highest
A
B
C
D
Lowest

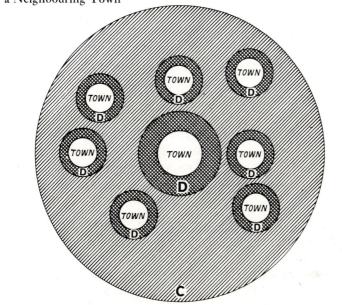

Fig. 17c   The Enclosure of the Spheres of Influence of Smaller Towns by the Larger Sphere of Influence of a Larger Town

interviewing people who are visiting the town for the purposes of obtaining various services (see page 11). These methods alone cannot be relied upon to provide a true picture of the sphere of influence of a town; they will tend to overestimate its extent. For example, suppose that on a given day a certain number of visitors have come to the town centre for shopping purposes. Some of these will have come from fairly distant villages, most of whose inhabitants perhaps normally shop in other competing towns. Hence, to say that a particular village is within the town's sphere of influence because a few shoppers visit the town on a particular day is an oversimplification. Referring to fig. 17b, a survey of the home locations of visitors to either of these towns could place the *whole* of the zone of competition within the sphere of influence of that town, which clearly would be inaccurate. Hence, investigations within the town can only indicate the approximate extent of its sphere of influence.

To complete the picture, field work has to be carried out *outside the town* near the estimated margin of the sphere of influence to try to fix the location of the social and economic 'watershed' between competing towns. Referring to fig. 17b, for example, field work would have to be carried out within the zone of competition between the two towns.

a) Field Work within the Town

i) Visits to Service Enterprises within the Town

Enterprises which may usefully be visited are:

1. Organizations which make deliveries of goods to the area surrounding the town. These include large shops, laundries, dry cleaners, etc. Also the local newspaper office may be able to provide information about the distribution area of the local newspaper.

2. Large industrial concerns may be able to provide information about the locations of the homes of their employees.

3. Local cultural societies may provide information about the area from which they draw their members.

In a short interview with a busy person it is difficult to obtain a clear picture of a particular service area. Hence it is wise to go equipped with a map of suitable scale. For a small enterprise which is likely to have only a small service area the 1 : 63 360 (one inch to one mile) Ordnance Survey map may suffice, but for a large enterprise with a wide service area a 'motoring' map on a scale 1 : 633 600 (10 miles to the inch) may be more useful.

It is important to guard against investigating a service enterprise which has an artificially restricted service area. It is often pointless, for example, to plot the locations of the homes of pupils in a school which is administered by a local education authority, since these pupils are obliged to live within the local authority boundary. For similar reasons, membership lists of local libraries are usually of little value, because residence within the local authority area is usually a requirement for library membership. Lending libraries run by commercial firms have no such restrictions of course.

ii) Central Area Street Questionnaires

Much valuable information about the sphere of influence of a town may be obtained by interviewing people who are visiting the town's central area for shopping or leisure purposes. This type of investigation is better carried out by a group of field workers than by a single student. Interviewers should be stationed along the major streets of the central area so that the whole area is covered as evenly as possible. Positions immediately outside a railway station or a bus station should be avoided because the sample of persons interviewed will tend to be rather biased in favour of certain settlements and districts. Care should be taken in planning the interview locations so as to avoid any kind of bias.

Each interviewer should conduct a particular number of interviews (say twenty). Shopping interviews are best carried out in the afternoon and leisure interviews in the early evening. It is a good idea to inform the local police force that interviews are going to be conducted.

The questionnaire should be as simple as possible. Examples are given below. In an interview, the interviewer should explain clearly and briefly the purpose of the interview and ask politely whether the person is willing to answer the questions. No pressure of any kind should be put on the interviewee. Most people are willing to answer questions if they are approached politely and they understand the purpose of the survey. After an interview is completed the questionnaire should be offered to the *next person* who passes the interview point.

Each questionnaire should be headed by the name of the school and should include a short statement such as: 'This school is conducting a survey of the shopping and other service facilities which are provided in (name of town). It would be helpful to our work if you would agree to answer the following questions.'

Shopping Questionnaire

1 Are you in _____ for the purpose of shopping? (If the answer is 'No' the interview should be concluded politely and the questionnaire offered to the next person to pass the interview point)

2 What is the name of the town or district in which you live? (This should be stated as clearly as possible, but the person's exact address is quite unnecessary and should not be asked)

3 Which of the following groups of goods are you intending to buy today? (i) Food, (ii) Clothes or footwear, (iii) Furniture, electrical goods or carpets.
   (The answer to this question may provide useful information concerning the service areas of particular groups of goods)

4 Where else apart from _____ do you shop for (i) Food? (ii) Clothes or footwear? (iii) Furniture, electrical goods or carpets?
   (This question, combined with Question 2, may provide useful information about the nature of competition for shoppers between towns)

5 How did you travel here today? (i) Foot, (ii) Car, (iii) Train, (iv) Bus, (v) Other.
   (This question may provide information about the nature of the transport links between the town and its surrounding area)

Leisure Questionnaire

This should have the same general form as the shopping questionnaire.

1 Are you in _____ for leisure purposes?
   (If the answer is 'No' the interview should be concluded politely and the questionnaire offered to the next person to pass the interview point)

2 What is the name of the town or district in which you live?
   (This should be stated as clearly as possible, but the person's exact address is quite unnecessary and should not be asked)

3 For what leisure activity are you in _____ this evening?
   (There are so many possibilities that a choice of a few groups cannot be offered. Useful information may emerge concerning the service areas of various types of leisure activities)

4 To which other town apart from _____ do you go for the leisure activity stated in the answer to Question 3 or for other leisure activities?
   (This question combined with question 2 may provide useful information about the nature of the competition between towns in terms of leisure activities)

5 How did you travel here this evening? (i) Foot, (ii) Car, (iii) Train, (iv) Bus, (v) Other.
   (This question may provide information about the nature of the transport links between the town and its surrounding area)

Both of these questionnaires are extremely short, but they may provide very useful information particularly when the answers to pairs of questions are considered together.

Pairs of Questions	Information Provided
2 and 3	Service areas for different groups of shopping goods and different leisure activities.
2 and 4	Competition between the town being surveyed and other towns in respect of shopping and leisure services.
2 and 5	Use of various transport facilities between the town being surveyed and different parts of its sphere of influence.

In addition, the answers to Question 2 alone will enable a map to be constructed which gives a general idea of the extent of the sphere of influence of the town.

b) Field Work outside the Town

For this type of survey, areas should be chosen which are situated near what is thought to be the outer margin of the town's sphere of influence and where there is likely to be a 'watershed' between the influence of the town being surveyed and another town or towns. A home interview survey may then be carried out by selecting perhaps every fifth or every tenth house (depending upon the size of the survey area) along the streets of the selected area. The aim of the survey is to measure the relative strengths of the influences of surrounding towns upon the survey area. An alternative method of investigating the sphere of influence of a town is explained in chapter nine.

Home Interview Questionnaire

The interviewer should explain clearly and briefly the purpose of the interview and should ask politely whether the person is willing to answer the questions. Each questionnaire should bear the name of the school and the explanatory statement suggested on page 77. (In the following questionnaire Town X refers to the town whose sphere of influence is being studied; Town Y refers to a possible competitor town)

1 For what type of shopping do you usually visit Town X?
(i) Food, (ii) Clothes or footwear, (iii) Furniture, electrical goods or carpets.

2 How often do you shop at Town X?
(i) Over once a week, (ii) Once a week, (iii) Once a fortnight, (iv) Once a month, (v) Less often.

3 At which other town in addition to Town X do you shop? (Assume that 'Town Y' is answered)

4 How often do you shop at Town Y (or other towns stated in reply to Question 3)?
(i) Over once a week, (ii) Once a week, (iii) Once a fortnight, (iv) Once a month, (v) Less often.

5 For what type of shopping do you usually visit Town Y (or other towns stated in reply to Question 3)?
(i) Food, (ii) Clothes or footwear, (iii) Furniture, electrical goods or carpets.

6 For what leisure activity do you usually visit Town X?
(There are so many possibilities that a choice of a few groups cannot be offered)

7 How often do you visit Town X for leisure activities?
(i) Over once a week, (ii) Once a week, (iii) Once a fortnight, (iv) Once a month, (v) Less often.

8 Which other town in addition to Town X do you visit for leisure activities? (Assume that 'Town Y' is answered)

9 How often do you visit Town Y (or other towns stated in reply to Question 8) for leisure activities?

10 For what leisure activity do you usually visit Town Y (or other towns stated in reply to Question 8)?

Here again, the answers to pairs of questions taken together will help to determine whether the interviewee is more strongly influenced by Town X or Town Y. The following pairs of questions will help to determine this: Question 1 and Question 5, Question 2 and Question 4, Question 6 and Question 10, Question 7 and Question 9.

Examples

a) Bolton

i) Visits to Service Enterprises within the Town

A visit was made to a large bakery located in Bolton and information was obtained concerning the extent of the firm's delivery areas for bread and cakes. Deliveries of bread are made daily; deliveries of cakes less frequently. The results are shown in fig. 18. Deliveries of bread are made over a large area, extending about sixty kilometres from north to south and roughly the same distance from east to west. The outline of the area is shown in fig. 18. Manchester and Salford are included in this area. Cakes are delivered over a rather larger area which extends north-west to Blackpool and Southport.

Membership lists of the Bolton and District branch of the Geographical Association have been used to compile fig. 19. Members of the branch are entitled to attend a total of approximately eight lecture meetings through the winter. Almost all branch members live within a radius of about twenty kilometres from Bolton. Other branches of the Geographical Association, providing roughly equivalent programmes of meetings, are located at Liverpool, Manchester, Blackburn and Blackpool. The service area in respect of sixth form conferences, which are held twice a year, is clearly considerably larger, and some school parties travel up to fifty kilometres to attend. On one occasion, a school travelled from the Birmingham district (considerably aided by the presence of the M6 motorway). The sixth form conferences, attendance at which is restricted to sixth form geography students, represent a more specialized service and therefore a service of higher status than the ordinary lecture meetings. Hence, it is not surprising that their service area is larger than the service area for ordinary membership of the branch.

ii) Central Area Street Interviews

Interviews were conducted with shoppers in the central area of Bolton. About seventy per cent. of all the shoppers interviewed lived within the county borough boundary; the remaining thirty per cent. lived in surrounding towns and villages. The locations of the homes of shoppers who lived outside the county borough boundary are shown in fig. 20a. The map shows that the great majority of shoppers from out of town lived within a radius of about nine kilometres from the centre of Bolton. It is likely that Bolton suffers competition in respect of shopping facilities from Blackburn (twenty kilometres away) to the north, Bury (nine kilometres away) to the east, Manchester (eighteen kilometres away) to the south-east,

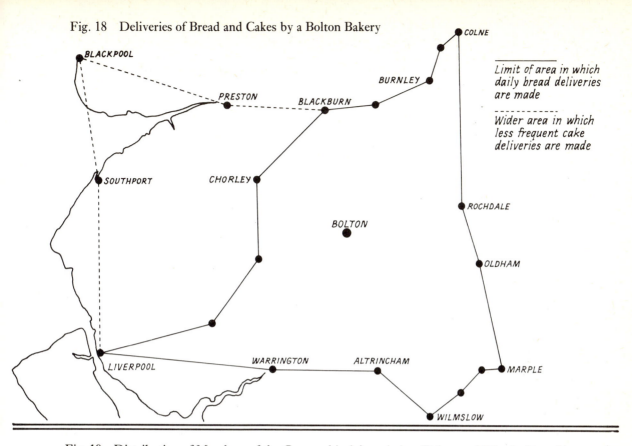

Fig. 18 Deliveries of Bread and Cakes by a Bolton Bakery

Limit of area in which daily bread deliveries are made

Wider area in which less frequent cake deliveries are made

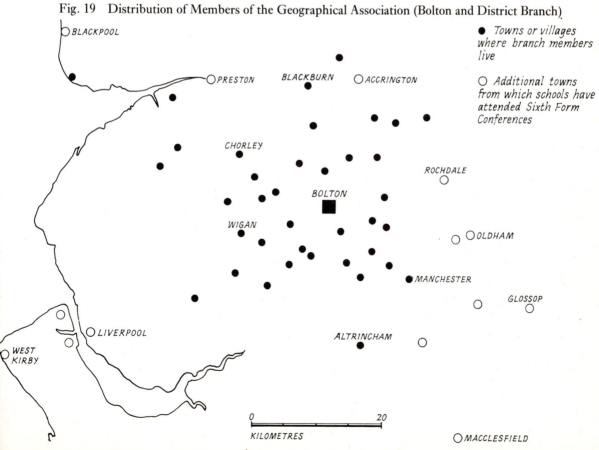

Fig. 19 Distribution of Members of the Geographical Association (Bolton and District Branch)

● Towns or villages where branch members live

○ Additional towns from which schools have attended Sixth Form Conferences

0   20
KILOMETRES

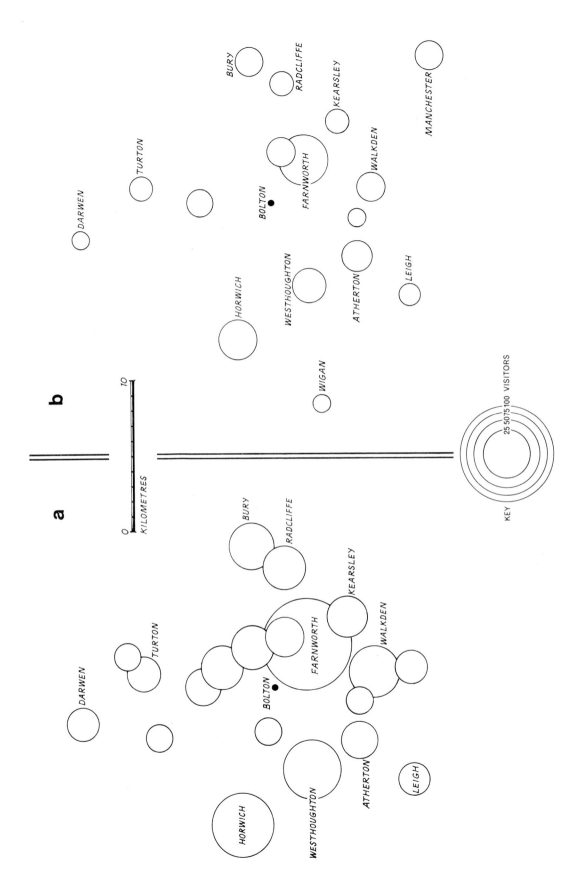

Fig. 20   The Home Locations of Persons Visiting Bolton for a) Shopping b) Leisure Activities

Wigan (sixteen kilometres away) to the west, and Leigh (thirteen kilometres away) to the south-west. Of these competitors Manchester is by far the largest and exerts the strongest influence.

Leisure interviews conducted in the central area of Bolton revealed that twenty two per cent. of interviewees lived outside the county borough boundary. The locations of their homes are shown in fig. 20b. The service area for leisure appears to be broadly similar to that for shopping, except that some interviewees had travelled from Wigan and Manchester.

b) Aberystwyth

A similar survey carried out in Aberystwyth revealed interesting contrasts with Bolton. Aberystwyth is a much smaller town than Bolton and the services it provides are generally of a lower status. On the other hand, Aberystwyth has few neighbouring towns of any size. The area surrounding Aberystwyth is the sparsely populated hill land of central Wales. Here are some of the results of this survey:

(a) People visiting the central area of Aberystwyth had travelled from a wide area with a radius of about thirty two kilometres extending from Machynlleth in the north to Lampeter in the south.

(b) Over forty per cent. of the interviewees lived outside Aberystwyth itself.

(c) Most of the interviewees (roughly seventy five per cent.) intended to shop for food.

(d) A striking contrast in shopping intentions existed between interviewees who lived in Aberystwyth itself and those who lived outside the town. Nearly thirty per cent. of the interviewees who lived outside Aberystwyth intended to shop for clothes or footwear, whereas less than twenty per cent. of Aberystwyth residents were shopping for these items.

(e) The interviews also suggested that Aberystwyth residents come under the influence of far distant but larger towns in respect of certain urban services. Few residents in the town normally shopped elsewhere for food, but considerable numbers visited Swansea, Cardiff and Shrewsbury for purchases of clothes, footwear and furniture. Similarly Cardiff and Swansea were visited for football matches. London theatres had been visited quite frequently.

Exercises

1 Construct a map showing the direction and frequency of bus services radiating from the centre of your town.

a) First draw a map showing the locations of the towns and villages to which bus services run from the centre of your town (the Ordnance Survey map of scale 1:63360 is useful for reference). Mark your town in the centre of the map.

b) Obtain timetables for all bus companies which serve your study area.

c) Choose a day of the week on which the flow of buses is not likely to be affected by any special event in the town – i.e. not a Saturday, Sunday, market day or early closing day.

For the chosen day, count the total number of buses (for all relevant companies) which travel between the major town and all other settlements in the chosen area.

d) Draw straight lines on your map from the town centre to the other towns and villages to show the broad pattern of the bus service network. Then vary the thickness of these lines in proportion to the number of bus journeys which are made along the various sections of each bus route.

In most cases, you will find that the number of bus journeys gradually decreases outwards from the centre of your town. This suggests that, as the distance from your town centre increases, its influence over the surrounding towns and villages becomes weaker.

A careful study of your completed map will suggest many ideas about the characteristics of the sphere of influence of your town.

2 Explain why the service areas illustrated in figs. 18 and 19 should not be regarded as realistic representations of Bolton's sphere of influence. An atlas map of south Lancashire will be useful.

3 a) Why is the service area for cakes (fig. 18) larger than that for bread?

b) Why is the service area for sixth form conferences (fig. 19) larger than that for Geographical Association branch membership?

4 Referring to an atlas map of south Lancashire discuss the extent to which figs. 20a and 20b are likely to be realistic representations of Bolton's sphere of influence. In which areas is it likely that home interview questionnaires would yield useful results? Give reasons.

5 a) From the information provided in this chapter, list the chief differences between the spheres of influence of Bolton and Aberystwyth. Using an atlas, explain the reasons for these contrasts.

b) Within the sample of persons who used Aberystwyth to purchase clothes and footwear, the proportion of shoppers from outside the town was greater than that of local resident shoppers. Explain this (see page 83).

9 The Field Study of Patterns of Service Centres and Spheres of Influence

This type of field work is best carried out in a rural area where there are a few towns and many villages, but no single town dominates the whole area. Thus, there is likely to be an interlocking pattern of spheres of influence covering the area.

General Principles

Service centres in a rural area are towns and villages which provide services, such as various types of shopping facilities and professional services, for the residents of the area. The type and status of service provided at any service centre generally depends upon the size of the service centre. Thus, a person who lives on a farm in a rural area may visit the nearest village shop if he wishes to buy food. If, on the other hand, he wishes to buy a new suit or to consult a solicitor, he may find that these facilities are not available in the village, so he will have to make a longer journey to the nearest small town. Should he wish to buy a large item of household equipment such as furniture, or to attend a theatre, he may not be able to satisfy his requirements in the nearest small town, which may only have a single small furniture shop and no theatre. Hence, he will need to

travel even further to a larger town which is able to provide a greater variety of services.

It can be seen therefore that larger service centres (i.e. large towns) provide a wider and fuller range of services than smaller settlements. The large centre will provide a wide variety of shops, including food shops, clothing shops, and a variety of shops selling household goods of all kinds. In addition the larger centre will provide a range of professional services, including banking and legal services, entertainment and personal services of many kinds. Such a service centre is said to be of high status or high order. Smaller towns will provide a more limited range of services. Here, there are still likely to be a number of food shops because food is frequently purchased, but there will be a smaller number and choice of clothing shops and shops selling large household goods such as furniture. Also, the range of other services may be narrower. A small town, for example, is almost certain to possess a doctor and at least one bank, but it is less likely to have a specialist optician or a theatre. Such a town is said to be of lower status than the larger town. Villages provide an even narrower range of services. The village will have fewer and a smaller variety of shops. There will often be at least one food shop, but clothing and furniture shops are usually absent. Similarly, the village may sometimes possess a doctor, but it is unlikely to have a bank.

It is possible therefore to arrange the service centres of an area in a list according to the number and variety of services which they provide (i.e. their status). The larger towns of high status will occur near the top of the list and the smaller villages of low status near the bottom of the list. Such a classification of service centres is known as a 'hierarchy of service centres'. Part of the purpose of studying patterns of service centres in the field is to measure their status and to recognize such a hierarchy.

Every service centre, whatever its position in the hierarchy, exists to provide services for its surrounding area or sphere of influence. A small village for example, will have only a small sphere of influence, represented approximately, perhaps, by the service area of the village shop or the doctor. A small town will have a larger sphere of influence which might be represented by the service area of its bank or its clothing shops. Thus, the small sphere of influence of the village in terms of the village shop is enclosed by the larger sphere of influence of the town measured, for instance, in terms of the bank. The situation is the same as is represented theoretically in fig. 17c except that we are now considering towns and villages instead of large towns and smaller towns. The sphere of influence of the large market town encloses all these smaller spheres of influence since it may be measured in terms of the service areas of high order services which probably do not exist in smaller service centres. Thus it can be seen that service centres of higher status tend to have larger spheres of influence than those of lower status and the larger spheres of influence enclose the smaller.

Theoretically one would expect the sphere of influence surrounding a town or village to be approximately circular in shape (figs.

17 and 21a). But if a large area is completely covered by the circular spheres of influence of several equally spaced towns it is inevitable that there is overlapping of adjacent circles. (fig. 21a). A zone of competition exists where adjacent circular spheres of influence overlap. (figs. 17b and 21a). If this zone of competition is assumed to be shared equally between each town and its neighbour, a pattern of hexagonal spheres of influence, completely covering the area, emerges (fig. 21b). Fig. 21b shows a simplified representation of this system.

The spheres of influence of the village centres shown on fig. 21b are represented in the form of small hexagons, the boundaries of the hexagons being placed half way between adjacent service centres which provide this 'village' grade of service. Clearly towns as well as villages are capable of providing 'village' services. Thus the whole area is covered with a patchwork of small hexagonal service areas.

Small market towns provide services of higher status which the villages cannot provide. Hence, the hexagons representing the spheres of influence of the small market towns, will reach out as far as the nearest set of villages, and will have their boundaries placed half way to the next small market town (fig. 21c).

The large market town provides services of higher status still. Hence, its sphere of influence is shown as extending outwards as far as the small market towns, and the boundaries of this hexagon are placed half way to the next large market towns (some of which are off the diagram). In fig. 21c, the large market town A has, therefore, three different service areas making up its sphere of influence. In terms of low status 'village' services it has a small hexagon just like the villages. In terms of services of the 'small market town' status, it has the same larger

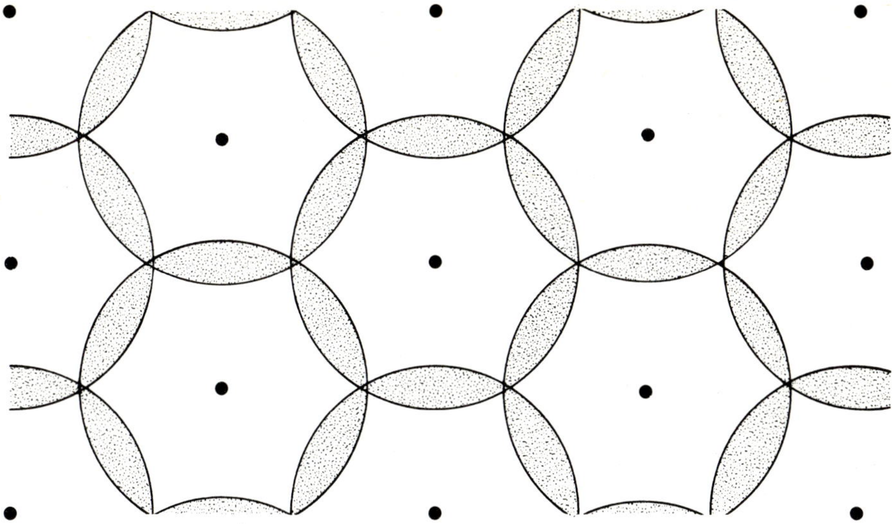

Fig. 21a Overlapping Circular Spheres of Influence with Zones of Competition

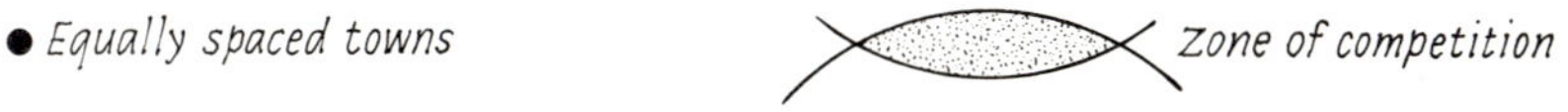

Equally spaced towns
Zone of competition

Fig. 21b Simple Hexagonal Pattern of Spheres of Influence

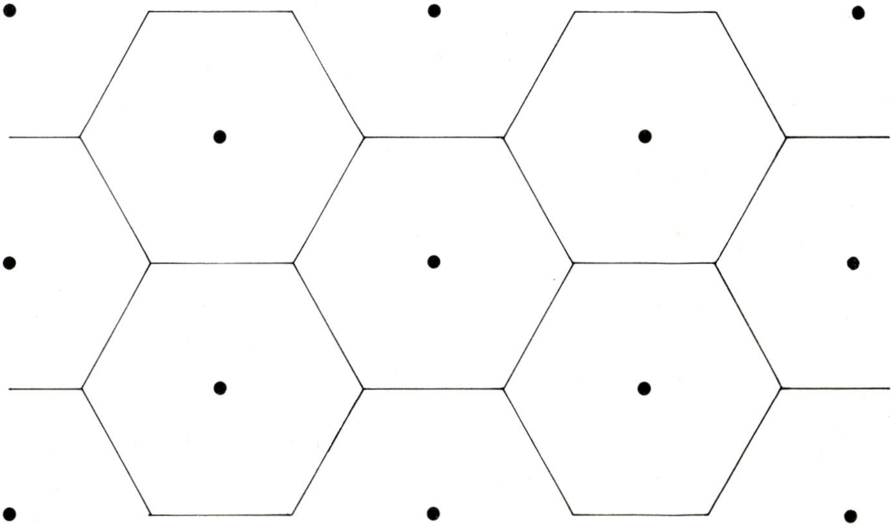

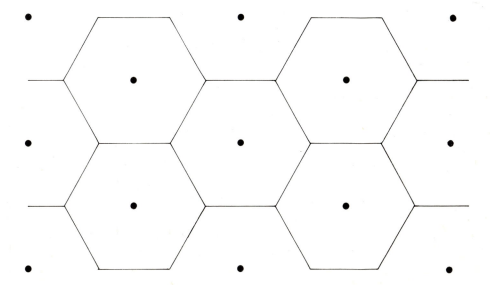

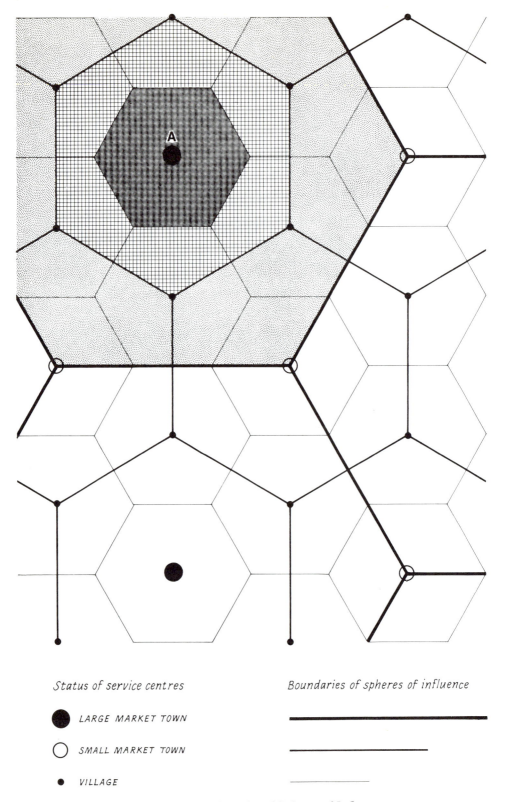

Status of service centres

● LARGE MARKET TOWN

○ SMALL MARKET TOWN

• VILLAGE

Boundaries of spheres of influence

Fig. 21c   The Hierarchy of Spheres of Influence

hexagon as the small market towns with which it competes for trade in the villages nearest to it. In terms of high status 'large market town' services, A's sphere of influence is shown as an even bigger hexagon which reaches out to the nearest small market towns, and completely encloses a number of village spheres of influence. Town A competes with other large market towns in all directions in terms of high status services.

The size of the sphere of influence of a service centre is bound to have an effect upon the length of the journeys which people make to it to obtain the services it provides. In the case of villages (fig. 21c) whose spheres of influence are small, journeys to the village are likely to be quite short. On the other hand, journeys to the large market town A (fig. 21c) may be very much longer because its sphere of influence is so much larger. Journeys to the villages are likely to be quite frequent since they will usually be concerned with the purchase of food or obtaining some other frequently demanded service. Visits to the large market town, on the other hand, are likely to be less frequent, since they will tend to be made for the purpose of buying clothes or furniture, or possibly attending a theatre or consulting a solicitor – all of which are services less frequently demanded.

Through the field study of these kinds of patterns, it will be possible to discover the extent and the nature of the spheres of influence of the different service centres of varying status which exist within the survey area.

Suggested Plan

Basically the field study is intended to discover:
a) the hierarchy of service centres in the survey area,

b) the sphere of influence of each service centre in the area.

a) The Hierarchy of Service Centres

The status of a service centre may be assessed by surveying the number and variety of services which it provides. To do this a count should be made of each of the following which may exist in the town or village:

i) Food Shops
These include all categories of shops from SS to S8 in the table on page 46. In addition, general village shops which sell a variety of goods including food, should be classified as food shops. Cafés and snack bars should not be included; these are service shops.

ii) Clothing Shops
These include categories S10, S11 and S12 (see page 46).

iii) Household Shops
These include categories S9, S13 to S27, S37 and S38 (see page 46). They are generally shops which sell furniture and miscellaneous household goods.

iv) Service Shops
These consist of categories S28 to S36 (see page 46).

Where a shop appears to have several functions, the main one should be selected. No shop must be counted twice. Petrol stations should be ignored.

v) Professional Services
The number of each of the following professional services which exist in the service centre should be counted: doctors, dentists, opticians, auctioneers, banks, solicitors and chemists.

In practice it is convenient to make out a logging sheet, as indicated overleaf, which will allow this information to be recorded neatly.

	Name of Town or village	
Food Shops		
Clothing Shops		
Household Shops		
Service Shops		
Total Shops		
Doctors		
Dentists		
Opticians		
Auctioneers		
Banks		
Solicitors		
Chemists		
Number of different types of professional service		

b) Spheres of Influence

The spheres of influence of the service centres in the survey area may be investigated by means of interviews carried out in each town or village. A total of five interviews, carried out with persons who actually live in each settlement, has been found to produce satisfactory results. In a more ambitious survey, it would be possible to vary the number of interviews in proportion to the approximate population of each settlement. No selection should be made of interviewees; when one interview is completed the field worker should try to interview the next person seen. In an interview, the interviewer should explain clearly and briefly the purpose of the interview and ask politely whether the person is willing to answer the questions.

The following questionnaire should be completed for five different people who live in each town or village:

1   Do you live in _____? (the town or village in which the interview is being carried out). If the person does not live in that village, the interview should be concluded politely and the next person seen should be interviewed.

2   Where (town or village only) did you last buy:
      (i) Bread? _____
   If bread is bought from a delivery van, state town or village in which the delivery bakery is located: _____
      (ii) Shoes? _____
      (iii) Furniture? _____

3   Where (town or village only) does your doctor live? _____

4   Where (town or village only) did you last visit a bank (not a post office)? _____

5   Where (town or village only) did you last visit a chemist?

    _____

The field work in each town or village, therefore, consists of (i) a count of shops and other services to complete the logging sheets, (ii) interviews conducted with five residents of the particular town or village to complete five copies of the questionnaire.

The processing of the information obtained will be discussed later.

Name of Settlement	NUMBER OF SHOPS					Number of Different Professional Services
	Food	Clothing	Household	Service	Total	
Hants/Dorset						
Ringwood	30	18	34	39	121	7
Blandford F.	33	17	36	14	100	7
Wimborne M.	24	17	32	16	89	7
Ferndown	21	10	16	20	67	7
Fordingbridge	15	6	15	7	43	6
West Moors	14	5	8	7	34	5
Parley Cross	9	2	4	4	19	3
Verwood	5	2	2	7	16	4
Cranborne	7	2	1	3	13	2
S.E. Lincs.						
Horncastle	32	20	39	21	112	7
Spilsby	22	15	9	17	63	7
Wainfleet A.S.	14	6	9	11	40	4
Burgh-le-M.	11	2	3	7	23	3
Chapel St. L.	5	3	4	5	17	3
Ingoldmells	11	1	5	6	23	2
Hogsthorpe	6	1	1	2	10	2
S.E. Devon						
Paignton	109	39	122	70	340	7
Newton Abbot	79	49	86	62	276	7
Totnes	44	16	49	31	140	6
Ashburton	23	5	12	9	49	6
Bovey Tracey	19	8	17	8	52	5
Kingsteignton	20	2	9	10	41	3
Kingskerswell	17	3	9	6	35	3
Buckfastleigh	8	4	12	6	30	3
Shaldon	13	2	7	7	29	3
Goodrington	5	1	3	4	13	3
Bishopsteignton	7	1	0	2	10	3

Table 3

Examples

The following examples of field studies were carried out on the borders of Hampshire and Dorset, a few kilometres inland from Bournemouth; in south-east Lincolnshire roughly between Skegness and Horncastle, and in south-east Devon a few kilometres inland of Torquay and Paignton.

a) The Hierarchy of Service Centres

First of all, a table is drawn up of the major service centres of the area from the information recorded on the logging sheets. (See Table 3).

It is fairly clear from this table that those service centres with large numbers of shops also have large numbers of different professional services. This relationship can be clearly illustrated in the form of a scatter graph using the 'Total Number of Shops' and 'Number of Different Professional Services' columns of the table (fig. 22). The general pattern of points on this scatter graph suggests that as the total number of shops increases, so does the number of professional services. From this graph, for example, one would expect a service centre with fewer than about thirty shops to have two or three different professional services. One would also expect service centres with more than about sixty shops to have the full range of seven professional services.

From Table 3 it is also possible to recognize the relative status of the service centres in each area by considering the number of different professional services each possesses, together with the number of shops. In Hants/Dorset, for example, it is easy to see that

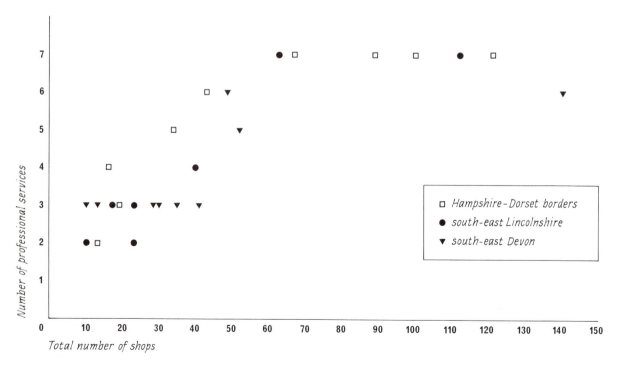

Fig. 22   A Scatter Graph of the Service Centres of the Hampshire-Dorset Border, South-east Lincolnshire and South-east Devon

Ringwood, with 121 shops and all seven professional services, has a higher status than Fordingbridge with forty three shops and six professional services. One can also recognize fairly close similarities between centres in different survey areas. Fordingbridge, for example, appears to be of similar status to Ashburton in S.E. Devon (forty nine shops and six professional services).

Information can also be derived from Table 3 about the relative status of the different types of shops. Graphs may be constructed relating 'Food Shops', 'Clothing Shops', 'Household Shops' and 'Service Shops' to 'Total Shops' (figs. 23a and b). These graphs indicate the different shop patterns in the various sizes of service centres. Fig. 23a, for example, indicates that through the whole range of service centres, food shops are more numerous than clothing shops, and food shops are particularly numerous in the service centres of low status in which clothing shops are particularly rare. A study of fig. 23b suggests that in service centres of low status which have few shops, service shops tend to be more numerous than household shops, whereas in larger service centres, household shops become relatively more numerous.

From the logging sheets it is also possible to arrive at conclusions concerning the relative status of the different types of professional services. In S.E. Devon, for example, doctors, chemists and banks are all found in quite small centres with less than forty shops, whereas solicitors, opticians, auctioneers and dentists only appear in the larger centres.

When the questionnaires have been processed, further information appears about the relative status of the various types of shops and professional services. Table 4 is constructed from the questionnaires and it shows the number of different service centres which interviewees as a whole had visited to make purchases of goods and to obtain professional services.

Furniture had last been bought in fewer centres than any other service, suggesting that only a few service centres in each area attract considerable numbers of furniture buyers, and that the selling of furniture is a service of fairly high status. Bread, on the other hand, had been bought in a large number of different service centres, suggesting that the sale of bread is a low status service which takes place even in quite small service centres.

Table 4

Total Numbers of Service Centres where Last Purchases or Last Visits had been made			
Service	S.E. Lincs.	S.E. Devon	Total
Bread	30	28	58
Shoes	11	8	19
Furniture	8	7	15
Doctor	14	19	33
Bank	15	10	25
Chemist	10	12	22

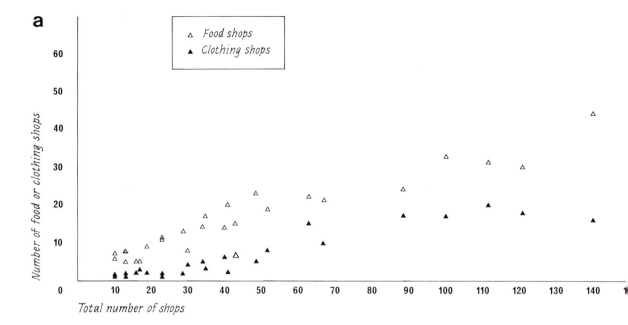

Fig. 23a   The Relationship between Food and Clothing Shops in the Service Centres of the
Hampshire-Dorset Border, South-east Lincolnshire and South-east Devon

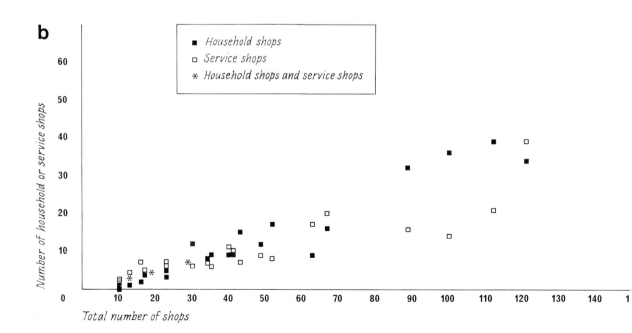

Fig. 23b   The Relationship between Household and Service Shops in the Service Centres of the
Hampshire-Dorset Border, South-east Lincolnshire and South-east Devon

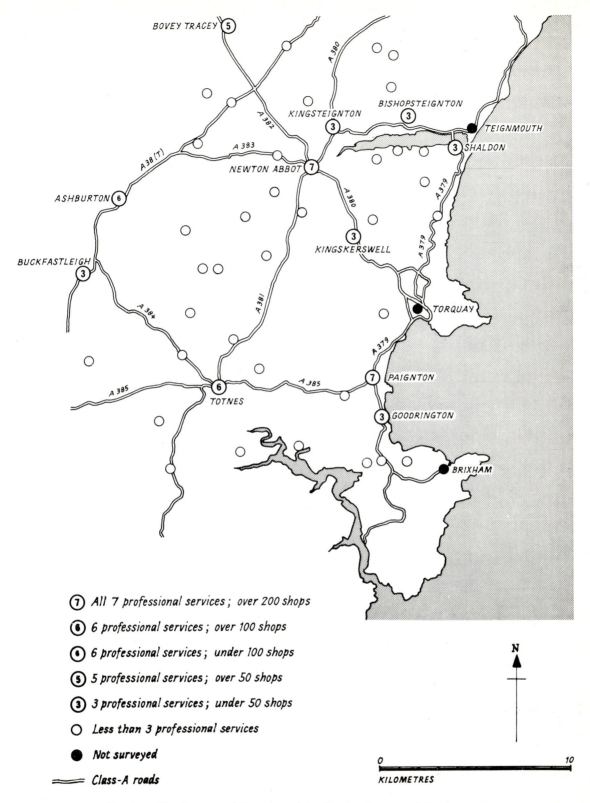

BOVEY TRACEY (5)

BISHOPSTEIGNTON
(3)

KINGSTEIGNTON
(3)

TEIGNMOUTH

SHALDON
(3)

NEWTON ABBOT
(7)

ASHBURTON (6)

KINGSKERSWELL
(3)

BUCKFASTLEIGH
(3)

TORQUAY

PAIGNTON
(7)

GOODRINGTON
(3)

TOTNES
(6)

BRIXHAM

A 380
A 382
A 383
A 38 (T)
A 379
A 380
A 379
A 379
A 384
A 381
A 385
A 385
A 379

N

(7) All 7 professional services ; over 200 shops

(6) 6 professional services ; over 100 shops

(6) 6 professional services ; under 100 shops

(5) 5 professional services ; over 50 shops

(3) 3 professional services ; under 50 shops

○ Less than 3 professional services

● Not surveyed

═══ Class-A roads

0   10
KILOMETRES

Fig. 24   The Status and Location of the Service Centres of South-east Devon

Finally, it is possible to divide the service centres of an area into groups according to their status as measured by the number of shops and the number of different types of professional services they possess. These different groups may then be plotted on an outline map of the area. (fig. 24). Their distribution should then be related to the information which is provided on the 1 : 63360 (one inch to one mile) Ordnance Survey map, such as the density of villages (hence approximate density of population), the pattern of communications etc. (fig. 24).

b) The Mapping of Spheres of Influence

Various aspects of the spheres of influence of the service centres may be discovered by the processing of the questionnaires. Three major stages are involved in this processing.

i) Mapping of the Information from the Questionnaires

Six tracings should be made from the 1 : 63 360 (one inch to one mile) Ordnance Survey map of the location of all the towns and villages in the survey area in which questionnaires were used. These six base maps are then used to map questionnaire information concerning last purchases of bread, shoes and furniture, locations of doctors and last visits to banks and chemists. On each map, the position of each town or village is indicated by a circle about two centimetres in diameter. After this preparatory work the actual mapping can begin.

On the first base map, the answers to the question 'Where did you last buy bread?' are plotted. If bread was bought from a delivery van, the location of the delivery bakery is taken as the answer to this question. The compilation of the map is somewhat laborious. For each questionnaire a line is drawn on the map from the place where the questionnaire was completed to the place where bread was last bought. All towns and villages to which people had travelled to buy bread or from which a delivery van had travelled are indicated by thickening the circle's circumference. Doing this will make clear on the completed map the direction in which people moved to buy their bread. There will be some cases in which an interviewee last bought bread in the village in which he lives. This is indicated by inserting a 'spoke' in the circle representing that village.

This process is carried out on the other base maps for each of the other items in the questionnaire. The finished maps give a striking impression of the links which appear to exist between village and village, and village and town.

Fig. 25 is an example of part of a completed map of this kind. In this diagram, it can be seen that five questionnaires have been completed in each centre. Some of the answers to these questionnaires are shown by lines running to other centres and some are shown by 'spokes' within the circle which represents the centre. The only centres to which interviewees had *travelled* to make their purchases are A, D and G. One can see, for example, that of the five people interviewed in centre B, four had last made their purchase in centre G and one in centre D. Also, three of the five interviewees who lived in centre H had last made their purchase in centre G, but the other two had made it in centre H itself.

It is a useful exercise to work out for yourself where the five residents of each of the following centres had last made their purchases: (i) centre E, (ii) centre M, (iii) centre K, (iv) centre G, (v) centre D.

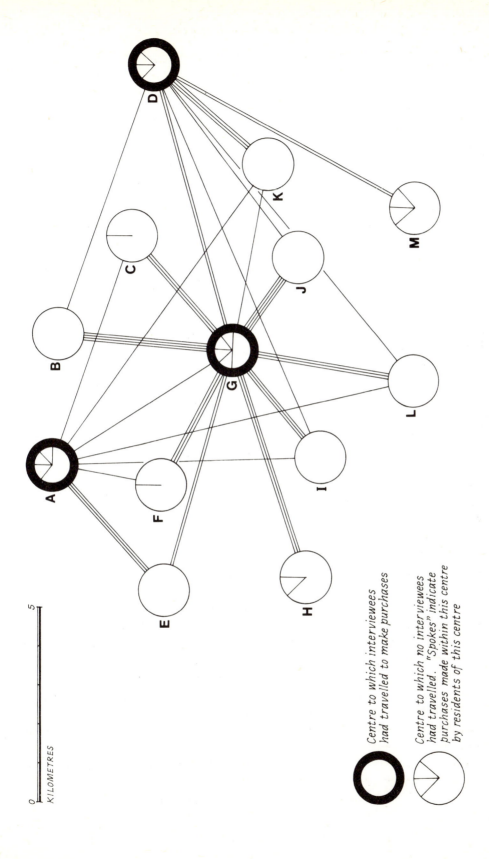

KILOMETRES

0   5

Centre to which interviewees
had travelled to make purchases

Centre to which no interviewees
had travelled. "Spokes" indicate
purchases made within this centre
by residents of this centre

Fig. 25   An Example of a Map Compiled from the Information from Questionnaires

Another useful exercise is to make lists of the centres from which some residents had travelled to make their purchases in: (i) centre G (eleven centres, omitting residents of G itself), (ii) centre A (six centres, omitting residents of A itself), (iii) centre D (six centres, omitting residents of D itself).

ii) Mapping of Major Service Links

The service maps completed as explained above are most striking in appearance and are well worthy of long and close study. Particular attention should be given to the contrasting patterns formed by the different services. Many conclusions are to be drawn from these. In their raw state however they are almost impossible to use for estimating spheres of influence, so the next step is to map their major characteristics. This process can be carried out on maps of a much smaller scale.

One map is allocated to each service as before, and towns and villages are indicated by small circles (figs. 26a, b, c, d, e and f). On each map the places to which people travelled to obtain the service are shown as solid circles, the other places being left open. Then, using the corresponding detailed map, a line is drawn on the new map from each town or village to the service centre where a *majority* of the interviewees last obtained the particular service. If equal numbers obtained the service at two or more service centres, a line is drawn to each service centre. A map is drawn in this way for each of the six services included in the questionnaire (fig. 26). These maps, in effect, will be a summary of the original detailed maps and the broad patterns they show. Although they are possibly less accurate, they are easier to understand. A selection of six such maps constructed for S.E. Lincolnshire is illustrated in fig. 26. A brief explanation of the patterns follows.

Last Purchases of Bread (fig. 26a). Bread sales had taken place in a large number of different centres. Bread of course is sold in nearly all villages. Thus, Burgh-le-Marsh, and Mareham-le-Fen, for example, seem to possess small service areas for bread sales. Superimposed upon the local service areas however, are the sets of longer lines, converging upon Skegness and going off northwards towards Grimsby. These indicate the sources and destinations of van deliveries.

Last Purchases of Shoes (fig. 26b). Here, the larger service centres appear to dominate. Skegness, Spilsby and Horncastle appear to have a strong influence over the whole area. There are signs of an attraction to Boston which lies about thirty kilometres to the south.

Last Purchases of Furniture (fig. 26c). The general pattern is much the same as that for shoes – Skegness, Spilsby and Horncastle again having important service areas. The main difference lies in the many lines which run off the map. The majority of these run to Boston to the south and Lincoln, which lies about thirty kilometres to the west of Horncastle. The selling of furniture is, as we have already seen, a service of high status, and it appears that people in this area are willing to make a longer journey to a larger service centre to obtain the benefit of a wider choice of furniture shops.

Locations of Doctors (fig. 26d). Most people appear to live fairly near their doctor and the map shows a neat set of compact service areas based upon a large number of different service centres.

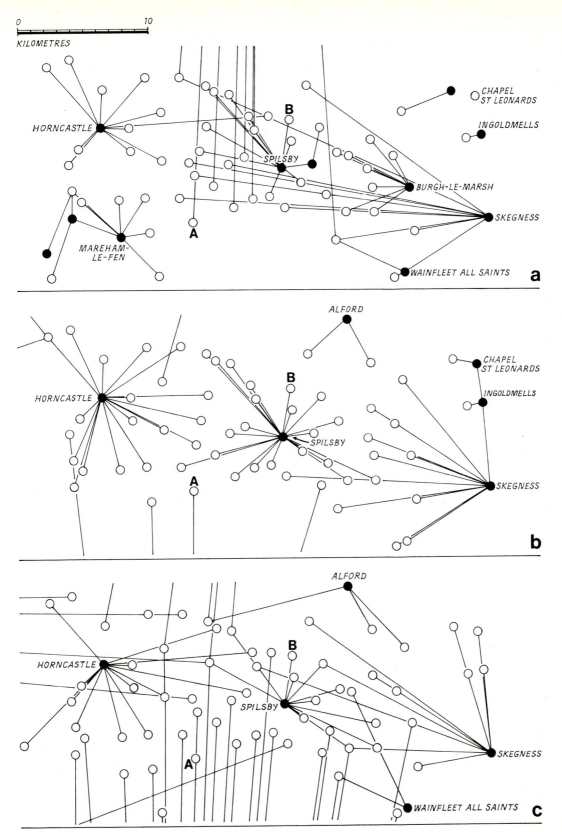

KILOMETRES
0   10

HORNCASTLE

B

SPILSBY

CHAPEL
ST LEONARDS

INGOLDMELLS

BURGH-LE-MARSH

SKEGNESS

MAREHAM-
LE-FEN

A

WAINFLEET ALL SAINTS

a

ALFORD

HORNCASTLE

B

SPILSBY

CHAPEL
ST LEONARDS

INGOLDMELLS

SKEGNESS

A

b

ALFORD

HORNCASTLE

B

SPILSBY

SKEGNESS

A

WAINFLEET ALL SAINTS

c

Fig. 26   Last Purchases of a) Bread b) Shoes and c) Furniture in South-east Lincolnshire

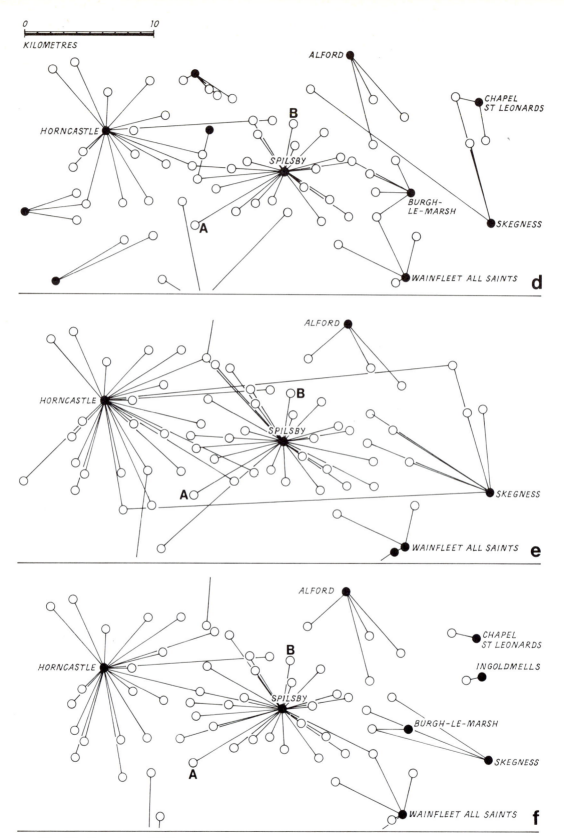

Fig. 26   Locations of d) Doctors and Last Visits to e) Banks and f) Chemists in South-east
Lincolnshire

Last Visits to Banks (fig. 26e). This is a typical 'market town' distribution, much resembling the map for last purchases of shoes. Skegness, Spilsby and Horncastle are important foci, and Wainfleet All Saints and Alford have smaller service areas.

Last Visits to Chemists (fig. 26f). This is generally similar to the 'bank' distribution except that Burgh-le-Marsh seems to interfere with the pattern near Skegness, and Chapel St. Leonards and Ingoldmells seem to have small service areas on the coast north of Skegness.

iii) Delimitation of Spheres of Influence
Each of the six maps in fig. 26 shows the main links between village and town for one particular service. A way of delimiting a possible sphere of influence is to take each village or town in turn and count its major service links with the various service centres on each map. If the village or town is linked in the majority of cases with a particular service centre, then it is regarded as being within the sphere of influence of that centre. The village marked A on the six maps in fig. 26, for example, is linked once with Grimsby (for bread), twice with Boston (for shoes and furniture) and three times with Spilsby (for

doctor, bank and chemist). A is therefore allocated to Spilsby's sphere of influence (fig. 27) – but only just! Village B (fig. 26) which has six links with Spilsby, appears to be more obviously within Spilsby's sphere of influence. This process is completed for every village or town in the area and a final map of spheres of influence is completed (fig. 27). Any villages which yield an indeterminate result when this process is applied to them are left blank. These tend only to occur on the margins of reasonably well-defined spheres of influence. Fig. 28 has been compiled in the same way for S.E. Devon.

c) Other Exercises Using the Base Maps

The six maps produced as explained on page 96 can be used for many other interesting studies.

A good exercise is to calculate the lengths of the journeys made to obtain the various services, assuming that the length of the journey is the distance along a straight line from home village to service centre. These measurements can be carried out quite quickly on the base maps of 1 : 63360 (one inch to one mile) scale. Statistics for the major service centres in S.E. Lincolnshire and S.E. Devon are given in Table 5.

Table 5

Service Centre	Average Distance Travelled to Obtain the Service (Kilometres)						
	Bread	Shoes	Furniture	Doctor	Bank	Chemist	All Services
Spilsby	5·39	4·99	5·33	4·67	5·51	5·34	5·18
Horncastle	5·51	6·41	6·58	6·18	5·99	6·05	6·12
Totnes	6·04	5·84	5·64	6·09	6·39	6·33	6·12
Newton Abbot	10·75	9·39	10·63	8·05	8·86	8·86	9·53
Paignton	8·69	6·23	8·74	6·33	6·18	7·08	7·13

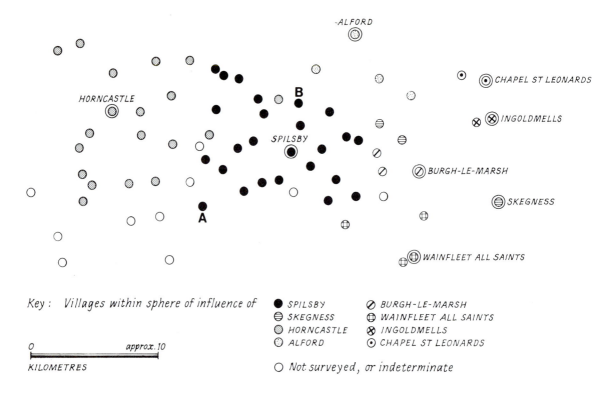

Fig. 27   Service Centres of South-east Lincolnshire – Spheres of Influence

Interesting graphs are produced when these quantities are plotted against total numbers of shops in the five service centres (figs. 29 and 30). In the smaller of the five service centres (Spilsby, Horncastle and Totnes) there is little difference between the six different services in terms of average journey length. Almost all these averages are between five and seven kilometres (fig. 29 and Table 5). In the case of the larger centres, Newton Abbot and Paignton, average journey lengths are generally greater and there is more difference between the average journey lengths in respect of the different services. Newton Abbot, with its very large sphere of influence (fig. 28) is a particularly interesting example in that it shows a correlation between the status of the services and the average distance travelled to obtain them. For example, journeys made to buy furniture, which is a high status commodity, have a higher average distance than journeys made to the town to visit a doctor – a low status service. The obvious exception to this correlation is seen in the case of bread (fig. 29). The high average distance of journeys made to buy bread in both Paignton and Newton Abbot is due to the fact that bakeries in these towns make widespread van deliveries throughout the surrounding area. If van deliveries were few or entirely absent, then the average journey distance for bread purchases would probably be the lowest recorded.

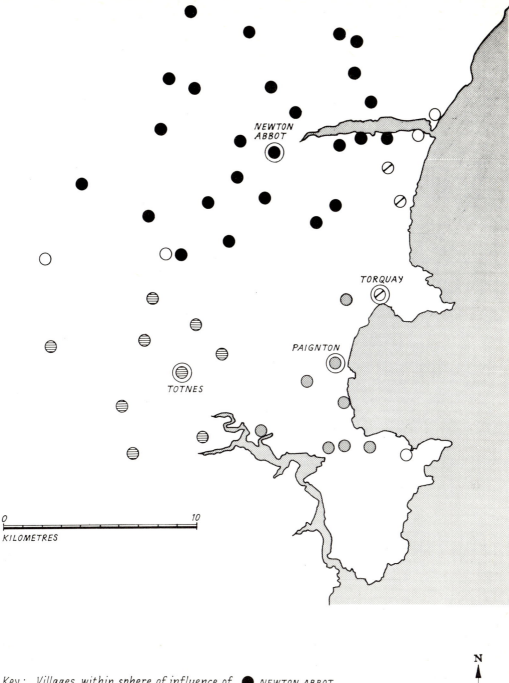

Key: Villages within sphere of influence of
● NEWTON ABBOT
⊖ TOTNES
◔ PAIGNTON
⊘ TORQUAY
○ Not surveyed, or indeterminate

Fig. 28   Service Centres of South-east Devon – Spheres of Influence

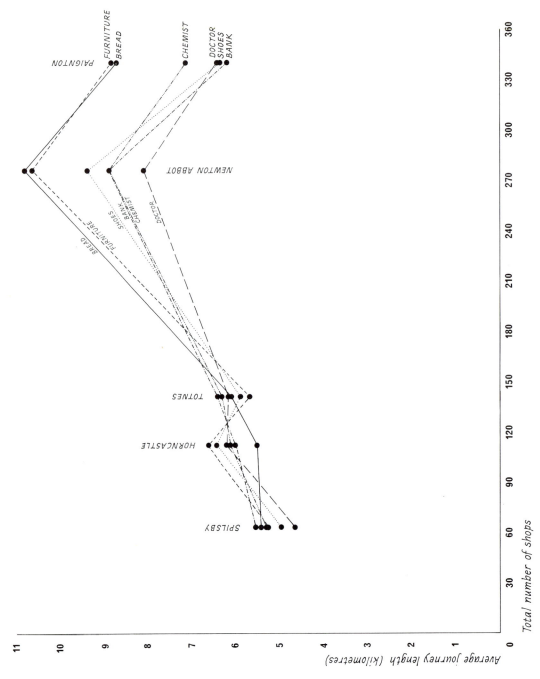

Fig. 29 A Graph of the Average Distance Travelled to Obtain Services in South-east Lincolnshire and South-east Devon

In fig. 30, the average journey length for all services is plotted against the size of the service centre. The graph shows that journeys tend to be longer to the larger service centres. This is, of course, related to the fact that, in general, the larger service centres have larger spheres of influence. Paignton, however, appears to be an exception. Although it has 340 shops, the average length of journeys to Paignton is relatively small. Fig. 28 also suggests that Paignton's sphere of influence is quite small in relation to the size of the service centre. It may well be that the function of most of Paignton's shops is to serve the population of the town itself rather than the population of surrounding settlements. A similar situation occurs in both Torquay (fig. 28) and Skegness (fig. 27). All three towns are holiday resorts and as such are subject to a large increase in population during the summer months. For the rest of the year the number of shops and services appears to be excessive for the requirements of the relatively small resident population.

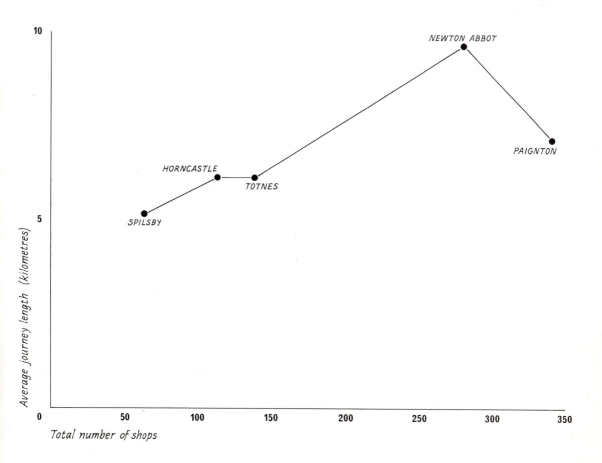

Fig. 30   A Graph of the Average Distance Travelled to Obtain all Services in South-east Lincoln-shire and South-east Devon

Exercises

1   How many different professional services (from the list used in this chapter) would you expect to find in a town of (a) fifty shops, (b) twenty shops? In each case, which services are likely to be present?

2   Referring to Table 3, state which service centres in S.E. Lincolnshire and S.E. Devon appear to resemble most closely the following service centres in Hampshire/Dorset. In each case comment on the similarities and differences. (a) Parley Cross, (b) Blandford Forum.

3   Refer to fig. 22. What appears to be the greatest difference between the service centres of S.E. Devon and those of Hampshire/Dorset and S.E. Lincolnshire.

4   Using figs. 23a and 23b, suggest how many food, clothing, household and service shops are likely to be possessed by service centres with (a) thirty eight shops, (b) fifty eight shops, (c) eighty shops. How many different professional services are likely to be present in each case?

5   Write a brief discussion of the patterns of service centres of varying status and the communications pattern in S.E. Devon (fig. 24).

6   Describe and explain the main differences between the service areas for bread sales (fig. 26a) and those for furniture sales (fig. 26c) in S.E. Lincolnshire.

7   Using figs. 26a to 26f, discuss the extent to which S.E. Lincolnshire appears to be a zone of competition between large service centres located outside the area. An atlas map will be useful.

8   Referring to figs. 26a to 26f and fig. 27, give as full a description and explanation as possible of the characteristics of the spheres of influence which have been delimited for (a) Alford, (b) Burgh-le-Marsh, (c) Spilsby, (d) Wainfleet All Saints.

9   Why do you think that the sphere of influence of Newton Abbot (fig. 28) extends further northwards and westwards than eastwards and southwards? Refer to an atlas map of S.E. Devon.

10 Using the information provided in this chapter, discuss the contention that holiday resorts have a relatively small social and economic influence on their surrounding areas. What kind of investigation would you design to attempt to discover the real extent of their influence?